THE ART OF THE DESSERT

Marc Chagall, *The Feast of Tabernacles*, 1907-1918

THREE HUNDRED DELIGHTFUL RECIPES
WITH FIFTY COLOR ART REPRODUCTIONS

The Art of the Dessert

SANDY LESBERG

PEEBLES
PRESS

Also by Sandy Lesberg

THE SINGLE CHEF'S COOKBOOK
SPECIALTY OF THE HOUSE
GREAT CLASSIC RECIPES OF EUROPE
GREAT CLASSIC RECIPES OF THE WORLD
A SHORT DRIVE IN THE COUNTRY
AT THE TABLE OF ISRAEL
THE ART OF AFRICAN COOKING

First Published 1977 by
Peebles Press International, Inc.
10 Columbus Circle, New York, New York 10019

DESIGNED BY NICOLAI CANETTI

© 1977 Peebles Press International, Inc.
ISBN 0-672-52327-2
Library of Congress Catalogue Card Number 76-53616

Distributed by
The Bobbs-Merrill Co., Inc.
4300 West 62nd St., Indianapolis, Indiana 42628, U.S.A.
in the United States and Canada

Barrie & Jenkins
24 Highbury Crescent
London N5 1RX, England
in the U.K., Ireland, Australia, New Zealand and South Africa

Printed and bound in the United States of America

TABLE OF CONTENTS

Maurice Utrillo, *Le Moulin de la Galette*, 1913-1915

Auguste Renoir, *A la Grenouillère,* 1879 (detail)

The Four Seasons, New York City
GENOISE
(French Sponge Cake)

    6 eggs
    6 egg yolks
    1 cup sugar
    1 cup sifted flour
    ½ cup clarified butter
    1 teaspoon vanilla extract

Combine eggs, egg yolks and sugar in a bowl. Set the bowl over a saucepan containing 1 or 2 inches of hot water. It should not touch the bowl and should never boil. Place over low heat and beat the mixture continuously as it warms. The eggs are warm enough when if you put your finger into them, not more than 1 drop falls from your finger, and the mixture looks like a bright, yellow syrup. Remove from the heat and beat with an electric mixer at high speed for about 15 minutes, or until the mixture becomes light, fluffy and cool. It will almost triple in bulk and will look very like whipped cream. Sprinkle the flour, a little at a time, over beaten eggs. Fold in gently, by hand. Add clarified butter and vanilla. Be very careful not to overmix or you will dissipate the air beaten in — which is what makes the Genoise light.

Pour the batter into whatever type of pan or pans required. This recipe yields two 9-inch or three 8-inch layers. Bake at 350° F. for 25 to 30 minutes, or until cake pulls away from pan and is golden brown. Remove from pans immediately and cool on a cake rack.

Serves: 8

Claude Monet, *Swamp with Water-lilies*, 1904

Nantes, France
GENOISE DE LA PROVINCE

  1 cup milk
  2 cups sifted all-purpose flour
  2 teaspoons baking powder
  ½ teaspoon salt
  6 eggs (at room temperature)
  2 cups granulated sugar
  1½ teaspoons vanilla extract
    Confectioners' sugar

In a small saucepan, heat milk just until bubbles form around edge of pan. Remove from heat; set aside. Preheat oven to 350° F. Sift flour with baking powder and salt; set aside. Beat eggs at high speed until thick and lemon-colored. Add sugar, beating until mixture is very thick. Blend in flour mixture at low speed until just smooth. Add warm milk and vanilla, beating until just combined.

Pour batter into an ungreased 13×9×2-inch baking pan. Bake until surface springs back to the touch — 35 to 40 minutes.

With cake still in pan, invert over cake rack and allow to cool completely; then gently remove from pan. Sprinkle lightly with confectioners' sugar and cut into squares.   *Serves: 10 to 12*

Maurice Utrillo, *The Artist's House in the Country*, 1933

The Tower Hotel, London
CHESTNUT GATEAU

8 eggs
1 cup sugar
1 cup flour
½ cup melted butter

Whisk eggs and sugar together with a balloon whisk in a bowl over a pan of hot water. Continue until mixture is light, creamy, double in bulk and shows the marks of the whisk. Fold in flour very gently, then fold in melted butter very gently.

Place batter in two 9-inch round, greased and floured Genoise molds and bake at 350° F. approximately 30 minutes. Let cake cool in the pan for 10 minutes before removing to a rack to finish cooling. When sponge is quite cold, slice into 2 layers.

Decoration

½ cup cream, whipped
3 meringues
1 cup chestnut purée
¼ cup butter
¼ cup sugar
2 tablespoons rum or kirsch
Crushed meringues
Marrons glacés

Fill layers with whipped cream and broken pieces of meringues. Re-form the gâteau and, using a pallet knife, coat the sides with a mixture of chestnut purée, butter, sugar and rum or kirsch, mixed together well until light and creamy. (Reserve 2 tablespoons for garnish.)

Decorate the sides with crushed meringues. Cover the top of the gâteau with fine threads of chestnut purée mixture. Place marrons glacés neatly around the top edge. *Serves: 12*

Raoul Dufy, *Concert in Orange*, 1948

York, England

FRESH-ORANGE SPONGE CAKE

    6 **eggs, separated**
1¾ **cups sifted all-purpose flour**
   ½ **teaspoon salt**
1½ **cups granulated sugar**
   1 **tablespoon grated orange peel**
   6 **tablespoons orange juice**
     Confectioners' sugar

Preheat oven to 350° F. Sift flour with salt; set aside. With electric mixer, beat egg whites at medium speed until just foamy throughout. Gradually beat in ½ cup of the granulated sugar, 2 tablespoons at a time, beating after each addition. Continue beating until stiff peaks form. Set aside.

In small bowl of electric mixer with same beaters, beat egg yolks at high speed until thick and lemon-colored. Gradually beat in remaining 1 cup sugar, beating until very thick. Beat in grated orange peel and juice. With wire whisk or rubber scraper, using an under-and-over motion, gently fold yolk and flour mixtures into egg white mixture until just combined.

Pour batter into an ungreased 10-inch tube pan. Bake at 350° F. until a cake tester inserted in center comes out clean — 35 to 40 minutes. Invert pan over cake rack and allow cake to cool completely in pan — about 1 hour. With spatula, carefully loosen sides of cake from pan; turn out on cake plate. Sprinkle top lightly with confectioners' sugar. *Serves: 8*

Vermeer, *View of Delft, c.* 1653

Jerusalem, Israel

YELLOW CAKE WITH MERINGUE

10 eggs, separated
1¾ cups sugar
4 tablespoons flour
1 teaspoon vanilla extract
½ teaspoon almond extract
2 tablespoons water

Beat egg yolks with 4 tablespoons sugar for 10 minutes. Add flour, vanilla and almond extract. Mix thoroughly and pour into a greased baking tin. Bake at 350° F. for 20 minutes.
While cake is baking, beat 1 cup of the sugar into egg whites until stiff. 5 minutes before cake is done, cover it with egg-white mixture and continue baking.

Brown remaining sugar in a saucepan. Add 2 tablespoons boiling water and remove from the flame. When cake is done and meringue is golden, pour on sugar mixture. Cool.

Serves: 8

Atlanta, Georgia

BUTTERMILK CAKE

2 cups sifted cake flour
1 teaspoon baking soda
½ teaspoon salt
⅔ cup shortening
1 cup sugar
½ teaspoon lemon extract
1 teaspoon vanilla extract
3 eggs, separated
½ cup buttermilk
3 tablespoons white distilled vinegar

Sift together flour, baking soda and salt. Cream shortening, sugar, lemon and vanilla thoroughly. Add egg yolks and continue creaming until mixture is light and fluffy. Add dry ingredients alternately with combined buttermilk and vinegar, adding dry ingredients first and last; beat thoroughly after additions.

(continued)

Beat egg whites until stiff but not dry; fold into batter.

Pour equal amounts of batter into each of two greased and floured 8×1½-inch round layer-cake pans or one greased and floured 11×7×-1½-inch loaf pan. Bake layers at 375° F. for 25 minutes; bake loaf at 350° F. for 40 to 45 minutes. Frost with lemon frosting. *Serves: 8*

Vermeer, *Street in Delft*, c. 1658

Henri Matisse, *Corn Poppies*, 1953

Jerusalem, Israel
HONEY CAKE

- 7 eggs, separated
- 1 cup sugar
- ¾ cup honey
- 2 cups flour, sifted
- 1 tablespoon orange rind, grated
- 1 teaspoon ground cloves
- ½ teaspoon cinnamon
- ⅛ teaspoon cardamom
- Dry brown sugar

Whip egg whites with half the sugar until stiff. Reserve. Beat egg yolks with remaining sugar and honey until light. Fold in whipped egg white mixture, flour, orange rind and spices.

Grease and flour a deep baking pan. Bake at 350° F. for 40 minutes. Set aside to cool. When cool, sprinkle with brown sugar.

Serves: 6

Jerusalem, Israel
HONEY-COCOA CAKE

- 2 cups sifted cake flour
- 1 teaspoon baking soda
- ½ cup cocoa
- 1 teaspoon salt
- ½ cup shortening
- ¾ cup sugar
- 1½ teaspoons vanilla extract
- ½ cup strained honey
- 2 eggs
- ⅓ cup milk
- ¼ cup vinegar

Sift together flour, baking soda, cocoa and salt. Cream together shortening, sugar, vanilla and honey thoroughly. Add eggs and beat until mixture is light and fluffy. Combine milk and vinegar. To the milk-vinegar mixture, add dry ingredients and creamed mixture in alternate small amounts, adding flour mixture first and last. Beat thoroughly after each addition.

Pour batter into 2 greased and floured 8×1½-inch round layer-cake pans. Bake at 350° F. for about 30 minutes. Cool 10 minutes. Remove from pans and cool completely. Frost with chocolate frosting.

Serves: 8

Henri Matisse, *Luxe, Calme et Volupté*, 1904

Ukraine, Soviet Union
SHANDOR HOLIDAY CAKE

1½ cups water
1 cup raisins
1 tablespoon baking soda
2 cups sugar
1 cup vegetable oil
3 eggs
1 teaspoon vanilla extract
¼ cup rum
2 teaspoons lemon juice
1 teaspoon lemon peels, grated
1 cup chopped walnuts
½ teaspoon salt
3 cups flour
Confectioners' sugar

Boil raisins in water for 5 minutes. Remove from heat, add soda and cool. Mix sugar, oil, eggs, vanilla, rum, lemon juice and lemon peels. When blended, add raisins and remaining water. Add nuts and salt. Blend in flour in three portions, stirring in completely after each addition.

Grease and dust with flour a bundt mold and pour in batter. Bake in preheated oven at 350° F. for 45 to 55 minutes, or until cake tests done with fork. Let cool in mold for 10 minutes, then turn out onto cake rack. Sprinkle top with a little confectioners' sugar. *Serves: 8 to 10*

London
BROWN VELVET

1½ cups sifted cake flour
¾ teaspoon baking soda
¼ teaspoon salt
2 squares (2 ounces)
    unsweetened chocolate
¼ cup shortening
3 tablespoons vinegar
¾ cup milk
1 cup sugar
1 egg, well beaten
1 teaspoon vanilla extract

Sift together flour, baking soda and salt. Melt together chocolate and shortening. Stir together vinegar, milk, sugar, egg and vanilla until sugar is completely dissolved. Add chocolate mixture and blend well. Stir in dry ingredients, about a third at a time, beating until smooth after each addition. This batter will be quite thin.

Pour into greased and floured 8×8×2-inch pan. Bake at 350° F. for 30 to 35 minutes. Frost with caramel icing.   *Serves: 8*

George Romney, *Lady Hamilton as Circé*

Chicago, Illinois
CHOCOLATE CAKE WITH EASE

2 cups sifted cake flour
1 teaspoon baking soda
½ teaspoon salt
¼ cup vinegar
¾ cup milk
1 teaspoon vanilla extract
2 eggs
¾ cup sugar
3 squares (3 ounces)
    unsweetened chocolate, melted
½ cup shortening

Sift together flour, baking soda and salt. Combine vinegar, milk and vanilla. Beat eggs, sugar and chocolate together for 1 minute at medium speed in electric mixer (or 150 strokes). Add flour mixture, shortening and half the liquid mixture. Stir until flour is dampened, then beat for 1 minute at medium speed, scraping sides of bowl often. Stir in remaining liquid mixture and beat at medium speed for 1 minute.

Pour into 2 greased and floured 8×1½-inch round layer-cake pans. Bake at 350° F. for 30 minutes. Frost with your favorite frosting.

Serves: 8

FUDGE CAKE WITH EASE

2 cups sifted cake flour
1 teaspoon baking soda
½ teaspoon salt
¼ cup vinegar
¾ cup milk
1 teaspoon vanilla extract
2 eggs
1½ cups brown sugar, firmly packed
2 squares (2 ounces) unsweetened
    chocolate, melted
½ cup shortening

Sift together flour, baking soda and salt. Combine vinegar, milk and vanilla. Beat eggs, sugar and melted chocolate together for 1 minute at medium speed in electric mixer (or 150 strokes). Add flour mixture, shortening and half the liquid mixture. Stir until flour is dampened, then beat for 1 minute at medium speed, scraping sides of bowl often. Stir in remaining liquid mixture and beat for 1 minute at medium speed.

Pour into greased and floured 13×9×2-inch pan. Bake at 350° F. for 45 minutes. Frost with your favorite frosting. *Serves: 8*

Richard Wilson, *The Thames at Twickenham*

Luca Signorelli, *Scene from the Life of St. Benedict*

Capucin Gourmand, Nancy, France
GATEAU DOMINIQUE

½ cup butter
½ cup sugar
2 eggs
2 teaspoons baking powder
1 teaspoon finely ground
    almond powder
½ cup flour
2 tablespoons raisins (sultanas),
    soaked in rum

Let butter soften in a bowl; then mix well with sugar. Add one whole egg, mix again; add the other egg, mix again. Sift baking powder with almond powder and flour and stir in well. Finally fold in soaked raisins.

Butter a 1½-quart mold and line bottom with buttered white paper. Pour batter carefully into mold and bake 30 minutes at 325° F.

Serves: 4

Pierre, Pau, France
LE GATEAU DES PRELATS
(Cake with Chocolate Mousse)

2 cups sugar
½ cup water
5 eggs
15 egg yolks
3½ squares (3½ ounces) baking chocolate,
  melted
2 cups heavy cream, whipped
12 ladyfingers or 1 layer sponge cake,
  thinly sliced
¼ cup strong coffee
  Additional melted bitter
    chocolate (optional)
  Brandied cherries (optional)
  Candied orange peel (optional)

Cook sugar and a scant ½ cup water until syrup forms a thin thread from end of spoon to pan. Cool syrup somewhat (about 200° F. on a candy thermometer). Add whole eggs and egg yolks, beating well with a wire whisk (you may find an electric mixer more satisfactory) until the mixture is completely cool. Add melted chocolate and mix thoroughly. Fold in whipped cream. Set aside.

Line a rectangular 2½-quart mold with some of the split ladyfingers or sponge-cake slices. Sprinkle with strong coffee. Spread chocolate mixture into mold and cover top with remaining ladyfingers or cake slices. Cover mold with waxed paper and refrigerate for 24 hours.

Unmold on a silver plate; pour more melted bitter chocolate over gâteau as a garnish, if desired. Flavor is also improved by decorating mold with cherries soaked in brandy or with candied orange peel. *Serves: 8*

Tel Aviv, Israel
BRANDIED CHOCOLATE CAKE

½ cup cocoa
¾ cup boiling water
1 teaspoon instant coffee
½ teaspoon Kaluaha brandy
  (coffee flavored)
1¾ cups flour
1¾ cups sugar
1 tablespoon baking powder
½ teaspoon salt
½ cup oil
7 eggs, separated
1 teaspoon almond extract
½ teaspoon cream of tartar

Dissolve cocoa in boiling water, stirring until no more bubbles form. Add instant coffee and brandy. Set aside. Combine flour, sugar, baking powder and salt. Make a hole in the center of these dry ingredients and pour in oil, egg yolks, almond extract and cocoa mixture. Blend thoroughly. Whip egg whites with cream of tartar until stiff. Fold into the prepared batter.

Transfer to a greased and floured baking pan. Bake at 350° F. for about 30 minutes, or until cake tests done. *Serves: 6*

MARBLE CAKE

         2 cups all-purpose flour
    3½ teaspoons baking powder,
            double acting
    1 teaspoon salt
    1¼ cups sugar
    ½ cup butter
    1 cup milk
    1 teaspoon vanilla extract
    2 eggs
    1 square (1 ounce) unsweetened
            chocolate, melted
    ½ teaspoon soda
    2 tablespoons hot water

With ingredients at room temperature, sift flour and resift with baking powder, salt and sugar 3 times. Add butter, milk and vanilla. Beat for 2 minutes. Scrape sides and bottom of bowl to combine well. Pour ⅔ of the batter into an 8 × 12-inch pan lined with paper.

Add cooled chocolate to remaining batter. Add soda dissolved in hot water. Beat for half of a minute. Run chocolate batter over light batter and cut a knife through several times for marble effect.

Bake at 350° F. for 35 minutes, or until cake tests done. Cool on rack before removing from pan. Cool thoroughly before frosting.

Serves: 10 to 12

CHOCOLATE CAKE

    5 eggs
    ¾ cup sugar
    ¾ cup flour
    6 tablespoons cocoa
        Sugar syrup (below)
        Garnish (below)
        Kirsch or rum
        Powdered sugar or chocolate curls

Break eggs into a bowl and whisk with sugar until smooth. Add flour and cocoa and mix. Put in a buttered and floured 10-inch baking tin and bake at 350° F. for 30 minutes, or until cake tests done. Meanwhile prepare sugar syrup and garnish (below).

Remove cake from oven and let cool. When cold, cut in 3 layers. Moisten layers with sugar syrup and a little kirsch or rum, then spread garnish over them and join together. Put garnish around sides and on top of cake. Sprinkle either powdered sugar or chocolate curls on top.

Sugar syrup

    ½ cup water
    1 cup sugar

Boil water and sugar for 10 minutes. Let cool.

Garnish

    ½ cup cream
    7 ounces (200 grams) melted chocolate

Bring cream to a boil. Add melted chocolate. Whisk cream and chocolate until thick, then cool.

Serves: 10

New York City
GATEAU D'AMOUR

12 eggs
1 cup sugar
1 cup flour
1 cup sweet butter
1 cup confectioners' sugar
½ cup Grand Marnier
2 cups heavy cream

Whip eggs and sugar until thick and foamy. When mixture clings to spoon, gradually add flour and continue to whip. Pour into a 14-inch or two 10-inch round pans which have been lightly buttered and sprinkled with flour. Bake 30 to 40 minutes in preheated oven at 300° F. When baked, set aside to cool.

To make a butter-cream spread, whip butter and confectioners' sugar until creamy. Set aside.

Meanwhile, prepare chocolate pudding (below).

After cakes have cooled, slice into 4 layers (3 layers if 14-inch pan is used) and cut into heart shapes. Sprinkle each layer with Grand Marnier. Place 1 layer on a plate and spread with butter cream. Alternate remaining layers with chocolate pudding and butter cream. Whip heavy cream until thick and spread over filled layers. Decorate to taste.

Chocolate Pudding

8-10 egg whites
2 cups sugar
½ pound (225 grams) bitter
    chocolate, melted
2-3 tablespoons whipped cream

Whip egg whites with sugar until stiff but not dry. Add melted chocolate and fold in whipped cream. This will make 2 cups of chocolate pudding.   *Serves: 16*

Brussels, Belgium
RED VELVET CAKE

2 cups flour, sifted
1 teaspoon baking soda
    Pinch of salt
2 squares (2 ounces)
    unsweetened chocolate
¾ cup butter
1½ cups sugar
2 eggs, beaten
2 teaspoons vanilla extract
2 tablespoons red food coloring
½ cup buttermilk
½ cup boiling water

Resift flour together with baking soda and salt. Melt chocolate in the top of a double boiler and set aside to cool. Cream butter until smooth and gradually add sugar, blending thoroughly. Beat in eggs until mixture is fluffy. Stir in vanilla and food coloring. Add flour mixture and buttermilk alternately in several portions, combining well after each addition. Pour in boiling water and beat until smooth.

Turn into two 8-inch layer-cake pans, lined with ungreased paper. Bake at 350° F. for 25 to 30 minutes, or until cake springs back when lightly touched. Remove from oven and allow to cool several minutes in pans before turning out on a rack.

When cool frost as desired.   *Serves: 8 to 10*

CHEESE CAKE SUPREME

Crust

    1½ cups graham-cracker crumbs
    ¼ cup brown sugar, firmly packed
    ½ teaspoon cinnamon
    ⅓ cup melted butter

Mix all ingredients until well combined and crumbly. Press evenly over bottom and sides of 9×9-inch baking pan.

Cheese cake filling

    2 eggs, slightly beaten
    ½ cup sugar
    1 teaspoon vanilla extract
    1½ cups creamed cottage cheese
    1 8-ounce package (225 grams)
       cream cheese, softened
    1 cup sour cream
    ½ teaspoon vanilla extract

Beat together eggs, sugar, 1 teaspoon vanilla, cottage cheese and cream cheese until smooth and creamy.

Pour into crumb-lined pan. Bake at 350° F. for 30 to 35 minutes, or until filling is evenly firm. Remove from oven and, while cake is still hot, spread with sour cream which has been flavored with ½ teaspoon vanilla. Chill in refrigerator at least 3 hours before serving.

Serves: 8 to 10

PINEAPPLE-CHEESE CAKE

    3 cups crushed pineapple
    1 package lemon-flavored gelatin
    ⅓ cup instant nonfat dry milk
    1 cup cottage cheese
    1½ cups graham-cracker crumbs

Drain pineapple, pressing out as much juice as possible into a separate bowl; reserve pineapple. Measure juice and add water, if necessary, to make 1 cup; heat to boiling point. Mix juice with gelatin; stir to dissolve; cool, chill until slightly thickened. Sprinkle dry milk over thickened gelatin. Whip at high speed on electric mixer until mixture is thick and light and has doubled in bulk. Fold in cheese and reserved pineapple.

Spread half the crumbs in a 9×9×2-inch pan. Alternate layers of pineapple-cheese mixture with remaining crumbs, ending with crumbs. Chill until set — about 2 hours. *Serves: 8*

FABULOUS COTTAGE CHEESE CAKE

1 6-ounce package (170 grams) Zwieback
½ cup confectioner's sugar
½ cup butter, melted
2 cups cottage cheese
4 eggs, separated
1 cup granulated sugar
¼ teaspoon salt
  Grated rind of 1 large lemon
  Juice of 1 large lemon
½ teaspoon vanilla extract
1 cup heavy cream
¼ cup sifted all-purpose flour

Grease an 8-inch spring-form pan heavily. Set aside. Roll the Zwieback into very fine crumbs. Coat the sides of the pan with the crumbs. Combine remaining crumbs with confectioners' sugar and melted butter. Press half on the bottom of the pan. Save remainder for cake top.

Force cottage cheese through a fine sieve (to break it up) into a very large bowl; beat egg yolks until thick and creamy, then gradually beat in ½ cup of the granulated sugar. Mix thoroughly with cottage cheese, salt, lemon rind, lemon juice, vanilla, heavy cream and flour. Beat egg whites until they stand in peaks when you hold up the beater, then gradually beat in remaining granulated sugar. Beat about a third into cheese mixture with a wire whisk. Fold in remainder carefully with a spatula.

Pour into prepared pan and cover top with remaining crumb mixture. Place in preheated 250° F. oven and bake for 1¾ hours. Leave in oven with heat off, door closed, until cake is cold. This helps to prevent cake from falling.

Serves: 8

Jerusalem, Israel
CHEESE CAKE WITH COGNAC

6 tablespoons margarine
1½-2 cups sugar
8 eggs, separated
2 pounds (900 grams) Ricotta cheese
1½ teaspoons vanilla extract
2 teaspoons cognac
2 tablespoons cornstarch
⅓ cup currants
4 tablespoons walnut meats
  Peel of 1 lemon, grated

Cream margarine and half the sugar. Beat egg yolks until light and add to margarine-sugar mixture. Beat in Ricotta cheese, vanilla, cognac, cornstarch, currants, walnuts and lemon peel. Combine thoroughly. Whip egg whites until stiff with remaining sugar. Fold into cheese mixture.

Bake in a greased and floured pan at 350° F. for approximately 1 hour.

Serves: 6

New York City
CHEESE CAKE CHERRY GLAZE

2 cups ripe sweet cherries
1 tablespoon sugar
¾ cup red currant jelly

Wash, stem and pit cherries. Simmer in water for 10 minutes. Drain and stir in sugar until dissolved.

In a saucepan beat currant jelly with a wire whisk to soften. Heat over very low heat (do not stir) until jelly is clear. Spoon several tablespoons out of the saucepan and set aside to cool. Add cherries to remaining jelly and gently coat with glaze. Spread the reserved tablespoons of jelly on top of cake, then mound on cherry mixture. Chill well before serving.

New York City
APPLESAUCE CAKE

1 cup seedless raisins
2 cups sifted all-purpose flour
1 teaspoon baking soda
1 teaspoon salt
1¼ teaspoons ground cinnamon
½ teaspoon ground allspice
¼ teaspoon ground cloves
½ cup shortening
1 cup sugar
1 egg
1 cup thick, sweetened applesauce
3 tablespoons vinegar

In a double boiler, steam raisins for 5 minutes. Cool. Sift together flour, baking soda, salt, cinnamon, allspice and cloves. Combine with raisins. Cream together shortening and sugar until fluffy. Beat in egg. Combine applesauce and vinegar. Add dry ingredients and applesauce mixture alternately to shortening-sugar mixture, adding dry ingredients first and last. Beat well after each addition.

Pour into greased and floured 9×9×1¾-inch baking pan. Bake at 350° F. for about 50 minutes. Frost with caramel icing.   *Serves: 8*

Mövenpick, Bern, Switzerland
CARROT CAKE

6 egg yolks
½ cup sugar
6 egg whites
¾ cup sugar
1½ cups finely ground hazelnuts
1½ cups scraped and shredded carrots
¼ cup flour
½ cup seedless raisins
1 teaspoon lemon extract
¼ cup lemon juice
1½ cups raspberry jam
¾ cup powdered sugar

Beat egg yolks and ½ cup sugar until frothy. Beat egg whites and ¾ cup sugar until stiff. Mix into the egg yolks, the hazelnuts, carrots, flour, raisins, lemon extract and lemon juice. Gently fold in the egg whites.

Pour into 2 lightly greased and floured 9-inch cake pans. Bake at 350° f. for about 30 minutes, or until cake begins to pull away from the pan or a tester comes out clean.

After the cakes have cooled, halve each of them and spread with raspberry jam. Replace the halves and sprinkle with powdered sugar.
Serves: 12

Jerusalem, Israel
ORANGE CAKE

1 orange, squeezed and unpeeled
1 cup currants
⅓ cup pecans, shelled
2 cups flour
¼ teaspoon club soda
1⅓ cups sugar
½ cup margarine
1 cup milk
2 eggs
5 tablespoons orange juice
1 tablespoon lemon juice
1 teaspoon cinnamon

Put orange, currants and pecans through the grinder. Combine flour, club soda and 1 cup of the sugar. Add margarine and ¾ cup milk. Mix for 2 minutes; add eggs and remaining milk and mix for 2 minutes more. Carefully incorporate orange-currant-pecan mixture.

Grease and flour a baking tin with margarine. Pour in batter and bake at 350° F. for 45 minutes.

Remove cake from oven and while it is still hot, pour on orange juice mixed with lemon juice. Sprinkle with remaining sugar, combined with cinnamon.

Serves: 6

Phoenix, Arizona
DATE-ORANGE CAKE

1 cup shortening
2 cups plus 2 tablespoons sugar
4 eggs
1½ cups buttermilk
1 teaspoon baking soda
½ teaspoon salt
4 cups flour, sifted
1 cup chopped dates
1 tablespoon grated orange rind
2 cups sugar
1 cup orange juice
Grated rind of 1 orange

Cream together shortening, 2 cups plus 2 tablespoons sugar and eggs. Stir in buttermilk. Sift together baking soda, salt and flour and combine well with mixture. Stir in chopped dates and grated orange rind.

Pour into a large, greased angel-food cake pan or bundt mold. Bake at 350° F. for 1¼ hours. Remove cake from oven and let stand for 10 minutes before inverting over a cake rack.

While cake is still hot, prepare the sauce: In a saucepan, bring 2 cups sugar, the orange juice and grated rind to a boil. Pour hot sauce immediately over hot cake. Allow cake to set until cold before serving.

Serves: 10

COCONUT-LEMON CAKE

1⅔ cups flour, sifted
1 cup sugar
½ teaspoon salt
3 teaspoons double-acting baking powder
½ cup shortening
½ cup coconut milk
¼ cup sweet milk
3 egg whites
1 teaspoon vanilla extract
½ teaspoon lemon juice
2½ cups freshly grated coconut

Ingredients should be at room temperature. Resift flour together with sugar, salt and baking powder into large bowl. Combine coconut milk and sweet milk and add half of this together with shortening to dry ingredients; beat 2 minutes on low speed with electric mixer (or 100 swift strokes by hand). Add remaining half of milk mixture together with egg whites, vanilla and lemon juice and beat again as above.

Turn into three 8-inch layer pans, lined with ungreased paper on the bottom. Bake at 350° F. for 18 to 20 minutes, or until cake tests done. Allow to cool in pans several minutes before turning out on a rack to cool completely.

Spread lemon filling (below) between layers and on top of cooled cake. Frost with icing (below) on top and sides. Coat with grated coconut immediately after frosting.

Lemon filling

½ cup flour
1⅔ cups sugar
½ teaspoon salt
⅔ cup water
4 egg yolks, beaten
1 tablespoon grated lemon rind
1 tablespoon freshly grated coconut
1 tablespoon red currant preserves
1 tablespoon butter
⅓ cup lemon juice

Combine flour, sugar and salt in saucepan and add water, stirring until smooth. Cook over moderate heat, stirring constantly, until thickened. Remove from heat and quickly beat in egg yolks. Return to heat and cook, stirring constantly, for 1 minute. Remove from heat and mix in lemon rind, coconut and currant preserves. Stir in butter and lemon juice until combined. Set aside to cool.

Icing

2 egg whites
¼ teaspoon cream of tartar
Pinch of salt
5 tablespoons cold water
1½ cups sugar
½ teaspoon vanilla extract
½ teaspoon lemon juice

Combine egg whites, cream of tartar, salt, cold water and sugar in the top of a double boiler over rapidly boiling water. Beat vigorously with a wire whisk for 8 minutes, or until icing stands in peaks. Place top of double boiler over ice water and add vanilla and lemon juice. Beat again until icing peaks. Immediately spread on cooled, assembled cake. *Serves: 8 to 10*

SWEET-POTATO CAKE

2 pounds (900 grams) sweet potatoes
½ cup margarine
1 cup brown sugar
  Juice of ½ lemon
½ teaspoon vanilla extract
¼ teaspoon almond extract
2 tablespoons cocoa
1 cup marshmallows, chopped
  Grated chocolate

Peel sweet potatoes and boil until tender. Drain. Transfer to a mixing bowl. Add margarine and brown sugar to sweet potatoes. Cover, let stand until margarine melts, then put sweet potato mixture through a food mill. Add lemon juice, vanilla and almond extract. Combine well. Divide the resulting mixture in half. Add cocoa to half the sweet potato mixture and beat until smooth. Stir in marshmallows. Reserve.

Spread a clean, damp towel on the table and spread half of the remaining sweet potato mixture (without the cocoa and marshmallows) on it. Reserve the remaining half. Cover with a second damp towel and press sweet potato mixture into a flat layer. Remove upper towel and cover the flattened layer of sweet potato with the sweet potato-cocoa-marshmallow mixture. Top with the reserved sweet potato.

Trim into a square or circle and turn out onto a platter. Sprinkle with grated chocolate. Refrigerate for 1 hour and serve.   *Serves: 6*

Monrovia, Liberia
PUMPKIN CAKE

½ cup shortening
1¼ cups sugar
2 eggs, beaten
2¼ cups cake flour
2 teaspoons baking powder
½ teaspoon salt
½ teaspoon cinnamon
½ teaspoon ginger
½ teaspoon nutmeg
1 cup cooked pumpkin
¾ cup milk
½ teaspoon baking soda
½ cup chopped nuts

Cream together shortening and sugar until fluffy. Add beaten eggs. In a separate bowl, sift together flour, baking powder, salt, cinnamon, ginger and nutmeg. In a separate bowl, mix pumpkin, milk and baking soda. Add flour mixture and pumpkin mixture alternately to shortening-sugar-egg mixture. Add nuts.

Pour batter into an 8-inch cake pan, lined with paper. Bake at 350° F. for about 50 minutes.
          Serves: 6 to 8

Vienna, Austria
APRICOT-PRUNE NUSSTORTE

¾ cup prunes
¾ cup apricots, dried
1 cup flour, sifted
½ teaspoon baking powder
¼ teaspoon salt
3 eggs, separated
1 cup granulated sugar
1 tablespoon milk
2 teaspoons rum
1 cup walnuts, chopped
   Whipped cream
8 walnut halves

Steam prunes and apricots for 15 minutes. Set aside to cool. Sift together flour, baking powder and salt. Beat egg yolks and beat in ½ cup of the sugar, the milk and rum. In a separate bowl, beat egg whites until they form soft peaks. Fold egg whites into yolk mixture. Add dry ingredients, a portion at a time, combining well after each addition. Fold in prunes, apricots and nuts.

Pour batter into an 8-inch cake pan, lined with greased paper and bake at 350° F. for 25 to 30 minutes. Allow to cool in pan for 10 minutes before inverting onto rack. Serve warm topped with whipped cream and walnut halves.

Serves: 8

Hotel Carlton Elite, Zürich
ENGADINER NUSSTORTE
(Engadine Nut Cake)

3½ cups flour
¾ cup butter
¾ cup sugar
½ cup margarine
1 egg
   Pinch of salt
1¼ cups sugar
2 cups heavy cream, warm
1¾ cups walnuts, coarsely chopped

Blend flour and butter until thoroughly mixed. Cream ¾ cup sugar and margarine, and beat in egg and salt until thoroughly blended. Chill.

While dough is chilling, caramelize 1¼ cups sugar and slowly heat cream. Add warm cream to caramelized sugar. Stir in walnuts.

Roll out half the dough to cover a 9-inch (2-inch deep) cake pan. Pour filling into cake pan. Cover with remaining dough. Pinch the edges together and prick lightly with fork. Bake at 350° F. for about 35 minutes, or until top is brown.

Serves: 6

¾ cup sherry
1 cup light raisins
1 cup dates, pitted and chopped
4 cups flour
2 teaspoons baking powder
½ teaspoon salt
½ teaspoon nutmeg
6 eggs
½ pound (225 grams) butter
1¾ cups granulated sugar
½ cup molasses
¼ cup orange juice
1 teaspoon vanilla extract
1 tablespoon grated orange rind
3 cups chopped walnuts

Add wine to raisins and dates and set aside. Sift together flour, baking powder, salt and nutmeg. Beat eggs until quite thick. In a very large bowl, cream butter and granulated sugar together until fluffy. Beat in eggs. Drain raisins and dates, reserving liquid. Combine reserved liquid with molasses and orange juice and add alternately with dry mixture to creamed mixture. Beat until smooth. Add vanilla, grated orange rind, raisins, dates and walnuts.

Spoon batter into a large tube pan lined with waxed paper. Bake at 275° F. for 2½ to 3 hours. Remove from oven and cool in pan for 10 minutes before turning out on a rack.

Meanwhile, prepare frosting (below). When cake is completely cool, frost the top generously and allow some to run down the sides.

Frosting

2 cups confectioners' sugar, well sifted
½ teaspoon vanilla extract
3 tablespoons water, approximate

Combine sugar and vanilla and add water to achieve desired consistency.

Serves: 10 to 12

2 cups sifted cake flour
1 teaspoon baking soda
½ teaspoon salt
1 teaspoon cinnamon
½ teaspoon ground cloves
½ teaspoon ground allspice
½ cup shortening
2 cups brown sugar, firmly packed
1 teaspoon vanilla extract
2 eggs
2 teaspoons vinegar
2 tablespoons sour cream
½ cup broken nut meats
Buttercream Frosting (see p. 184)

Sift together flour, baking soda, salt, cinnamon, cloves and allspice. Cream together shortening, sugar and vanilla thoroughly. Add eggs, beating well after each addition. Add dry ingredients and combined vinegar and sour cream alternately to the creamed mixture, adding dry ingredients first and last, beating well after each addition. Fold in nut meats.

Pour batter into 2 greased and floured 9×1½-inch round layer-cake pans. Bake at 375° F. for 25 to 30 minutes. Frost with Buttercream Frosting.

Serves: 8

Copenhagen, Denmark
TIVOLI CAKE
WITH RASPBERRIES OR PEACHES

1 cup flour, sifted
½ cup butter, creamed
⅓ cup confectioners' sugar
1 egg yolk, slightly beaten
1 teaspoon vanilla extract
½ cup heavy cream

Sift flour into a bowl and make a well in the center. Combine butter, sugar, egg yolk and vanilla separately and then pour into the well. Working with hands, knead into a smooth dough using small amounts of flour at a time. Chill for 30 minutes.

On an ungreased baking sheet, shape dough into a circle (¼-inch thick and 8 inches in diameter). Edges should be even. Bake in a preheated 375° F. oven for 12 minutes, or until cake is golden (not brown). Remove from oven and set aside to cool.

Meanwhile, prepare raspberry or peach topping (below).

Brush thin coating of desired glaze on top of cooled cake.

Arrange raspberries or peaches attractively on top and gently brush on remaining glaze.

Whip heavy cream until quite stiff and pipe around edge of fruit-covered cake.

Raspberry topping

2 cups fresh, whole raspberries
¾ cup red currant jelly

Carefully wash and dry berries. To make a glaze, beat currant jelly with a wire whisk to soften. Heat in a saucepan over very low heat (do not stir) until jelly is clear. Remove from heat.

Peach topping

4 fresh, ripe peaches
¾ cup apricot jam
2 teaspoons lemon juice
1-2 teaspoons water

Wash, peel and uniformly slice peaches. (If not ripe, simmer peach slices in water for 5 minutes. Drain and set aside to cool.) To make a glaze, force apricot jam through a sieve into a saucepan. Add lemon juice and water and bring to a boil. Simmer for several minutes, sieve once again and reheat. *Serves: 8*

Milwaukee, Wisconsin
RASPBERRY BAVARIAN CAKE

Batter for Fresh-Orange Sponge Cake (see p. 9)
1 cup boiling water
1 package raspberry-flavored gelatin
1½ cups fresh, ripe raspberries
1 cup sifted confectioners' sugar
⅔ cup evaporated milk (1 small can)

Prepare batter for Fresh-Orange Sponge Cake as directed. Pour into an ungreased 8-inch (deep dish) cake pan. Bake at 350° F. for 35 minutes, or until cake tester inserted in center comes out clean. Invert over cake rack and allow to cool in pan for 1 hour. Carefully loosen sides of cake from pan and remove. Set aside.

Add boiling water to gelatin; stir to dissolve; cool. Add raspberries and sugar to cooled gelatin and chill until slightly thickened. Pour evaporated milk into shallow pan and chill in freezer until ice crystals form around edge. Remove from freezer and whip milk in small bowl until stiff; fold into thickened gelatin.

Cut cake horizontally into 4 thin layers. Spread raspberry mixture between layers and on top of cake. *Serves: 8*

ORANGE CHIFFON CAKE

2¼ cups sifted cake flour
1½ cups sugar
3 teaspoons baking powder
1 teaspoon salt
½ cup vegetable oil
5 egg yolks, unbeaten
  Grated rind of 2 oranges
  Juice of 2 oranges
1 cup egg whites
½ teaspoon cream of tartar

Sift together flour, sugar, baking powder and salt into a mixing bowl. Make well in center of sifted ingredients and add oil, egg yolks and orange rind. Measure orange juice and add enough water to make ¾ cup liquid; add to mixture. Beat mixture by hand until smooth. In a large bowl, whip egg whites and cream of tartar until stiff peaks form. Pour first mixture over egg-white mixture and fold gently just until blended.

Pour into an ungreased 10-inch tube pan. Bake at 325° F. for 1 hour. Remove from oven and with cake still in pan, invert pan over a cake rack until cool.

Orange Sauce

6 egg yolks
1 cup sugar
1 cup orange juice
1½ tablespoons orange rind
2 cups heavy cream
½ cup pecans, chopped

In the top of a double boiler, combine egg yolks, sugar, orange juice and rind. Place over hot, not boiling, water and cook until mixture is thickened, stirring occasionally. Remove from heat and set aside to cool. Whip the cream and add cooled orange mixture. Stir in chopped pecans and serve over cake.   *Serves: 8*

KLM FIRST CLASS RUM CAKE

1 10-inch ring pound cake
Orange juice
Jamaican rum

Soak cake briefly in a solution of orange juice and rum. When placing on the serving tray, spoon some additional rum on top of cake. Reserve soaking solution. Fill center hole with orange-cream filling (below).

Orange-cream filling

2 cups milk
6 tablespoons sugar
2 oranges
4 tablespoons cornstarch, approximate
½ cup whipped cream
1 banana, sliced
½ cup canned peaches, sliced
½ cup canned pears, sliced
½ cup fresh strawberries, halved
3 tablespoons Jamaican rum

Bring milk to a boil with 4 tablespoons of the sugar and grated peel of the 2 oranges (reserve orange juice). Thicken mixture with half of the cornstarch; chill. When cold, whip mixture and add 2 tablespoons of the whipped cream and the reserved orange juice. Spoon filling into hole, level with top of cake.

Decorate with sliced bananas, peaches, pears and strawberries. Bring reserved soaking solution to a boil and thicken with remaining cornstarch. Clarify by adding remaining 2 tablespoons of sugar and the rum. Spoon this over entire cake while still hot. Just before serving, pipe on remaining whipped cream.

Serves: 8 to 10

YULETIDE FRUITCAKE

1 cup dark raisins
1 cup golden raisins
¾ cup dried figs, sliced
¾ cup dried apricots, chopped
1 cup diced citron
1 cup candied cherries, sliced
1½ cups walnuts, chopped
4 teaspoons cinnamon
1 teaspoon ground cloves
Pinch of pepper
1 tablespoon rum
½ cup orange marmalade
⅓ cup sweet sherry
1½ cups butter
1 cup sugar
4 eggs
3 cups flour
1 teaspoon baking powder
½ teaspoon baking soda
2 teaspoons salt

Mix together fruits, nuts, spices, rum, marmalade and sherry. Cream butter and sugar, beating until light. Add eggs, one at a time, beating thoroughly after each. Sift together flour, baking powder, soda and salt. Combine dry ingredients with creamed mixture and fruit mixture. Pour batter into 2 greased loaf pans.

Topping

½ cup golden raisins
¼ cup dried apricots, chopped
½ cup citron, sliced
½ cup candied cherries, halved
1 cup chopped walnuts
¼ cup honey
1 tablespoon rum
Pinch of cinnamon
Pinch of ground cloves

Combine all ingredients to serve as a topping on the fruitcake before baking.

Cover and bake at 250° F. for 3 hours. (Place a pan filled with water in the oven to keep cake from drying.) Remove from oven and let cool for 10 minutes before unmolding on a rack. Cool and wrap tightly in foil for storage. Cakes may be kept in the freezer for several weeks.

Yield: 2 fruitcakes

HALF-YEAR FRUITCAKE

½ cup sugar
½ cup shortening
3 eggs
1¼ cups flour
½ teaspoon salt
½ teaspoon baking powder
1 cup candied cherries, halved
1 cup candied pineapple, chopped
1 cup dates, pitted and chopped
1 cup golden raisins
1 cup slivered almonds
Corn syrup

In a large bowl, combine sugar, shortening and eggs and beat well. Sift together flour, salt, and baking powder and stir into mixture. Mix in remaining ingredients.

Pour batter into a greased 9×5-inch loaf pan, lined with waxed paper. Bake at 300° F. for 1¼ to 1½ hours, or until a fork inserted in center comes out clean. Let stand several hours until cool; remove from pan and peel off paper. Glaze with corn syrup and wrap tightly in foil. This fruitcake will keep up to a half year in refrigerator.

Yield: 1 fruitcake

STREUSEL CAKE

1½ cups all-purpose flour
¼ teaspoon salt
2 teaspoons baking powder
¼ cup butter
⅓ cup sugar
1 egg
⅔ cup milk
½ teaspoon vanilla extract
1 teaspoon grated lemon peel
Softened butter

Sift flour and resift with salt and baking powder. Cream butter and add sugar. Continue creaming until well blended. Beat in egg and milk. Combine both mixtures and add vanilla and lemon gratings, stirring until smooth. Spread batter in a greased 9-inch pan. Butter top of batter.

Streusel topping

2½ tablespoons flour
2½ tablespoons hard butter
3 tablespoons sugar
2 tablespoons brown sugar, firmly packed
Cinnamon
Nutmeg
Sliced almonds (optional)

Combine flour, butter and sugars until crumbly. Sprinkle over top of batter. Sprinkle cinnamon and nutmeg lightly on top and almonds, if desired.

Bake at 375° F. for 25 minutes. Cool on rack.

Serves: 8 to 10

Vancouver, British Columbia
CHOCOLATE-PEPPERMINT REFRIGERATOR CAKE

1 package ladyfingers (about 16), split
½ teaspoon unflavored gelatin
½ package (4 ounces) chocolate pudding and pie-filling mix
½ square (½ ounce) unsweetened chocolate
¾ cup milk
¼ cup crushed peppermint candy
½ cup heavy cream, whipped

Line a 9×5×3-inch pan with half of the ladyfingers. In a saucepan, combine gelatin, pie-filling mix, chocolate and milk. Cook according to package directions. Pour hot chocolate mixture in a bowl; stir in crushed candy. Place piece of waxed paper directly on top of pudding to prevent film from forming; cool thoroughly. Fold in whipped cream.

Spoon half the mixture into ladyfinger-lined loaf pan; cover with layer of ladyfingers. Spoon remaining chocolate mixture over ladyfingers. Refrigerate until set — about 4 hours. To serve, cut into slices.

Serves: 3 to 4

CHOCOLATE BLANC MANGE
ROLL CAKE

1 cup flour
1 teaspoon double-acting baking powder
¼ teaspoon salt
5 eggs, separated
1 cup sugar
2 teaspoons vanilla extract
  Confectioners' sugar (for coating)

Resift flour together with baking powder and salt. Beat egg yolks well and gradually add ½ cup of the sugar and the vanilla, beating until fluffy. Beat egg whites until fluffy, add remaining sugar gradually and beat until quite stiff. Combine egg-yolk mixture into whites and add dry ingredients in several portions.

Spread batter into a shallow baking pan lined with greased paper. Bake at 375° F. for 12 minutes, or until cake tests done.

Carefully invert on a towel covered with confectioners' sugar. (If cake edges are crisp, cut off.) Working quickly while cake is still hot, roll up width-wise; wrap towel around; allow to cool.

When cool, unroll and spread with filling (below). Re-roll, dust with confectioners' sugar and wrap in waxed paper or foil. Chill in refrigerator at least one hour before serving.

Blanc Mange filling

1 tablespoon unflavored gelatin
¼ cup cold water
1 square (1 ounce) unsweetened chocolate
1 tablespoon water
⅓ cup sugar
  Pinch of salt
½ cup plus 2 tablespoons light cream
1 teaspoon vanilla extract
½ cup heavy cream

Soften gelatin in the cold water. Melt chocolate in the top of a double boiler over hot, not boiling, water. Add the 1 tablespoon water and stir in sugar and salt. Add cream and cook until thickened, stirring constantly. Add gelatin and heat until dissolved. Remove from heat and add vanilla. Chill until partially firm.

Whip heavy cream until quite stiff and fold into filling mixture. *Serves: 10*

Brauereigaststätte Aying, Aying, West Germany

APPLE COOKIES WITH APRICOT SAUCE

1 teaspoon yeast
4 egg whites, beaten frothy
½ cup milk, lukewarm
2 cups sifted flour
1 teaspoon salt
4 egg yolks, beaten
2 tablespoons olive oil
1 cup water
4 apples, peeled and sliced
½ cup cinnamon-sugar
1 cup apricot marmalade or preserves
¼ cup white wine

Dissolve yeast in egg whites and milk. Mix flour and salt together. Beat in egg yolks and then oil. Work in water until flour mixture is thick but soupy. Let stand for 15 minutes. Fold in egg white-yeast mixture and then apple slices.

Pour into a flat, greased pan and bake at 325° F. until dough is browned and puffy. Remove from oven. Cut into squares and dip in cinnamon-sugar.

Heat apricot marmalade and white wine together. When mixture is like syrup, place apple cookies on dessert plates and pour sauce over them.   *Yield: 1 dozen*

Bath, England

LEMON COOKIES

3 cups sifted all-purpose flour
⅓ cup sugar
2 tablespoons baking soda
¼ teaspoon salt
⅔ cup shortening
1 teaspoon grated lemon rind
½ teaspoon lemon extract
1 tablespoon vinegar
¼ cup milk

Sift together flour, sugar, baking soda and salt. Cut in shortening with pastry blender or fork until fine. Add grated lemon rind and blend together. Combine lemon extract, vinegar and milk; add to flour mixture, blending well.

Roll on lightly floured board to ⅛-inch thickness. Cut into fancy shapes with cookie cutters. Place on cookie sheet. Prick with fork. Bake at 400° F. for 12 minutes.   *Yield: 4 dozen*

Charleston, South Carolina
MOLASSES COOKIES

1½ cups sifted flour
¼ teaspoon baking soda
⅓ teaspoon salt
½ teaspoon ground ginger
¼ teaspoon cinnamon
⅛ teaspoon nutmeg
⅛ teaspoon ground cloves
½ cup shortening
¼ cup dark-brown sugar, firmly packed
¼ cup molasses
1 egg
½ tablespoon vinegar

Sift together flour, baking soda, salt, ginger, cinnamon, nutmeg and cloves. Cream shortening and sugar until fluffy. Add molasses, egg and vinegar and beat until smooth and light. Add dry ingredients to shortening mixture in several portions, stirring until smooth after each addition. Chill dough for 1 or 2 hours.

Divide dough into 3 portions and shape each into a roll about 2 inches in diameter. Wrap each roll in waxed paper and chill overnight.

Slice ⅛ to ¼-inch thickness and place on cookie sheet. Bake at 350° F. for 10 minutes.

Yield: 4 dozen

Chicago, Illinois
OVENLESS CHOCOLATE PEANUT-BUTTER COOKIES

½ cup milk
2 cups sugar
3 tablespoons cocoa
¼ pound (110 grams) butter
3 tablespoons peanut butter
3 cups quick-cooking rolled oats, uncooked
1 teaspoon vanilla extract

In a large saucepan, combine milk, sugar, cocoa, butter and peanut butter. Heat to boiling point, stirring frequently to combine peanut butter. Continue to boil for 1½ minutes. Remove from heat and stir in remaining ingredients, being careful that oats are well distributed in mixture.

Using a teaspoon, drop dough onto waxed paper and allow to cool and firm.

Yield: 3 dozen

Edinburgh, Scotland
OATMEAL CRISPS

¼ pound (110 grams) butter
1 cup brown sugar, firmly packed
1 cup flour
½ teaspoon salt
½ teaspoon baking soda
1½ cups oatmeal
3 tablespoons water

Cream together butter and brown sugar. Sift together flour, salt and baking soda and mix in with butter and sugar. Add oatmeal and mix well. Finally, add water and mix thoroughly.

Lightly grease a cookie sheet and drop batter from spoon onto sheet. Pat down batter with a knife. Bake at 375° F. for 12 minutes. Remove cookies from baking sheet and place, while still hot, into a cookie tin (not on waxed paper).

Yield: 2 dozen

Boston, Massachusetts
CRANBERRY DROP COOKIES

½ cup butter
1 cup granulated sugar
¾ cup brown sugar, firmly packed
1 cup milk
2 tablespoons orange juice
2 eggs
3 cups sifted flour
1 teaspoon baking powder
¼ teaspoon baking soda
1 teaspoon salt
1 cup walnuts or pecans, chopped
2½ cups cranberries, coarsely chopped

Cream together butter and sugars. Beat in milk, orange juice and eggs. Sift together flour, baking powder, baking soda and salt and add to creamed mixture. Stir in nuts and cranberries.

Drop by teaspoonfuls onto a greased cookie sheet. Bake at 375° F. for about 10 minutes.

Yield: 6 dozen

Honolulu, Hawaii
COCONUT CHIP DROPS

1 cup sifted all-purpose flour
⅛ teaspoon baking soda
⅛ teaspoon salt
2 eggs
1¼ cups brown sugar, firmly packed
½ teaspoon vanilla extract
½ tablespoon vinegar
½ tablespoon melted butter or margarine
1¼ squares (1¼ ounces) unsweetened
    chocolate, chopped
½ cup chopped pecans
½ cup chopped coconut

Sift together flour, baking soda and salt. Beat eggs, brown sugar and vanilla together until thick. Stir in vinegar and melted butter or margarine. Blend in dry ingredients, chocolate, nuts and coconut.

Drop by teaspoonfuls onto cookie sheet. Bake at 375° F. until lightly browned — about 10 minutes. Cool on cake rack.

Yield: 1½ to 2 dozen

Vienna, Austria
LEBKUCHEN
(Gingerbread Cookies)

2 cups flour
¾ cup sugar
2 eggs, beaten
1 cup honey
1 teaspoon baking soda
¼ teaspoon ginger
¼ teaspoon cinnamon
¼ teaspoon powdered cloves
1 egg, beaten

Work all ingredients except beaten egg into a dough. Roll out to ¼-inch thickness. Cut into various shapes with cookie cutter. Brush with beaten egg.

Bake on greased and floured cookie sheet at 350° F. for 15 to 20 minutes.

Note: Instead of brushing with egg, top cookies with light coating of powdered-sugar icing flavored with lemon juice. *Yield: 3 to 4 dozen*

Honolulu, Hawaii
CHINESE ALMOND COOKIES

        1 cup sugar
    1½ cups shortening
        3 cups pastry flour
    ¼ teaspoon baking soda
    ½ teaspoon salt
        2 teaspoons almond extract
        1 egg, beaten
    ½ cup almonds, finely chopped
        Almond halves

Cream sugar and shortening. Add flour, soda and salt; mix well. Blend in almond extract, egg and chopped almonds. Shape dough into round balls and flatten. Place an almond half in center of each cookie.

Bake at 350° F. for 10 minutes, or until lightly browned. Allow cookies to cool several minutes before removing from baking sheet.

Yield: 4 dozen

Jerusalem, Israel
TANGY CARROT COOKIES

        2 cups flour
    ¼ teaspoon salt
    ½ teaspoon ginger
        1 cup margarine
    ⅓ cup sugar
        2 eggs, beaten
    ⅓ cup orange juice
        1 teaspoon lemon rind, grated
    ½ teaspoon vanilla extract
    ⅓ cup grated carrots

Sift together flour, salt and ginger. Cream together margarine and sugar, then beat in eggs. Add orange juice, grated lemon rind, vanilla and grated carrots. Stir in flour mixture to make a fairly stiff dough.

For cookies, place teaspoonfuls of dough on a greased baking sheet and bake at 350° F. for about 10 minutes.

The dough may also be rolled out, filled with cheese filling (below), rolled closed, dipped in flour and baked at 350° F. until brown.

Cheese filling

    1½ pounds (675 grams) cream
        cheese, softened
    ½ cup milk
        2 eggs, separated
    ⅓ cup sugar
        2 tablespoons dates, chopped
    ½ teaspoon vanilla extract
        1 tablespoon flour

Combine softened cream cheese and milk. Add egg yolks. Whip egg whites with sugar and stir in. Add remaining ingredients and mix well.

Yield: 2 dozen

36 THE ART OF THE DESSERT

COOKIES

Tel Aviv, Israel
TEHINA AND NUT BALLS

Tehina

> 4 tablespoons semi-prepared *tehina*
> (a paste made of crushed sesame seeds,
> available at specialty shops in jars and
> cans in semi-prepared form)
> Juice of 1 lemon
> ½ cup water
> ½ teaspoon salt
> 5 garlic cloves, crushed

Blend together semi-prepared *tehina* and lemon juice. Add water, bit by bit, until resulting mixture has the consistency of sour cream. Use more water if necessary. Add salt and garlic.

Filling

> 1 pound (450 grams) walnuts, ground
> 2 tablespoons dates, chopped
> 6 tablespoons sesame seeds
> 1 teaspoon cinnamon

Combine all ingredients together with prepared *tehina* to make a smooth mixture.

Dough

> 6 cups flour
> 2 cups margarine
> ½ cup sugar
> ½ cup warm water
> ¼ teaspoon salt
> 1 egg yolk, beaten
> Sesame seeds

Combine flour, margarine, sugar, water and salt and knead into a dough. Divide dough into 4-inch squares or circles. Fill each section with 1 tablespoon filling, seal closed and flatten between the palms of your hand.

Arrange in a greased baking tin, coat with beaten egg yolk, sprinkle with sesame seeds and bake at 350° F. for 30 minutes.

Yield: 1½ dozen

Tel Aviv, Israel
NUT COOKIES

> 1 pound (450 grams) walnuts, ground
> 1½ cups brown sugar
> 5 grains cardamom, freshly ground
> Pinch of ground cloves
> ½ teaspoon lemon juice
> 2 egg whites
> ½ cup apple juice
> 2 tablespoons potato flour

Combine walnuts, sugar, cardamom, cloves, lemon juice and egg whites. Work into a smooth dough. If dough is too stiff, thin with apple juice.

Form dough into small balls and place on a baking sheet dusted with potato flour. Bake for 15 minutes at 350° F.

Yield: 2 dozen

PORCUPINES

1¼ cups sifted all-purpose flour
⅛ teaspoon baking soda
¼ teaspoon salt
½ cup butter
¼ cup sugar
1¼ teaspoons vanilla extract
½ tablespoon vinegar
12 dates, pitted
1 egg, slightly beaten
1¼ cups puffed rice

Sift together flour, baking soda and salt. Cream butter and sugar until fluffy. Add vanilla and vinegar. Add dry ingredients gradually, blending well after each addition. Cover and chill for 2 hours.

Cut dates in half crosswise. Shape dough into 1-inch balls, wrapping around half a pitted date. Dip balls in slightly beaten egg and roll in puffed rice. Bake on cookie sheet at 350° F. for about 18 minutes. *Yield: 2 dozen*

RUM NUT SQUARES

Puff paste
6 tablespoons margarine, melted

Roll out puff paste and divide into two 12-inch squares. Place the first square on a greased baking sheet and cover with all the filling (below). Top with the remaining square of paste.

Indent top layer of paste with a sharp knife to form thirty-six 2-inch squares. Coat with melted margarine. Bake at 325° F. until the top layer is golden. Remove from oven. Separate squares with a knife and cover with syrup (below) immediately.

Filling

1½ cups walnuts, crushed
¼ cup brown sugar
¼ teaspoon nutmeg, freshly ground
¼ teaspoon cinnamon

Combine the above ingredients thoroughly.

Syrup

2 cups sugar
1 cup water
1 teaspoon lemon juice
Rum to taste

Bring sugar and water to a boil. Add lemon juice. Continue to cook, stirring constantly, until syrup thickens. Remove from heat and flavor with rum to taste. *Yield: 3 dozen*

MAKROUDH
(Date Squares)

Tunis, Tunisia

1 pound (450 grams) Alig (or local) dates
2 cups olive oil
½ teaspoon cinnamon
2¾ pounds (1¼ kilograms)
    coarse semolina
1½ tablespoons salt
Warm water
Sugar
Juice of 1 lemon

Wash and dry dates carefully and remove stones. Mash dates to a smooth paste with ½ cup of the oil and ½ teaspoon cinnamon. Heat remainder of the oil slightly. Measure semolina into a fairly large bowl and pour heated oil over, adding salt. Using a little warm water, mix dough to a fairly stiff consistency.

Roll out on oiled board to ½-inch thickness and cut in strips 3 inches wide. Place a ribbon of date paste, ½-inch thick, down the middle of each strip of dough. Fold over dough and bring edges together.

A flat, engraved wooden mold (about 2 feet long and 3 inches wide) is used to press a pattern onto the surface of the *makroudh* dough. Press this mold or similar form firmly onto the strips of date-filled dough to flatten them to a thickness of ½ inch and trim off edges with a knife.

Cut into squares and bake at 375° F. for 25 to 30 minutes. Prepare a syrup from warm water and sugar, flavored with lemon juice. Dip the *makroudh* squares in the syrup and leave to drain. *Serves: 8 to 10*

COCOA-NUT FINGERS

New Orleans, Louisiana

1 cup flour, sifted
¼ teaspoon baking powder
½ teaspoon salt
⅓ cup cocoa
¼ cup butter, softened
1 cup sugar
2 eggs, beaten
1 teaspoon vanilla extract
¼ cup milk
⅓ cup moist raisins
¼ cup walnuts, chopped

Sift flour with baking powder, salt and cocoa. Cream butter and gradually add sugar, continuing to cream until thoroughly mixed. Add eggs and vanilla and beat well. Add dry ingredients in several portions alternately with milk, stirring well after each addition. Stir in raisins and chopped walnuts.

Spread batter into a greased 11×7×1½-inch pan. Bake at 350° F. for 20 to 25 minutes. Cool in pan for 15 minutes, then cut into "finger" shapes. *Yield: 1 to 1½ dozen*

DOUBLE-FROSTED BOURBON BROWNIES

Lexington, Kentucky

½ cup confectioners' sugar
⅓ cup shortening
2 tablespoons water
¾ cup semisweet chocolate morsels
1 teaspoon vanilla extract
2 eggs
¾ cup sifted cake flour
¼ teaspoon baking soda
¼ teaspoon salt
1½ cups coarsely chopped walnuts
⅓ cup bourbon
　White frosting
　Chocolate Glaze (see p. 184)

Combine sugar, shortening and water; cook over low heat to boiling point, stirring constantly. Remove from heat. Add chocolate morsels and vanilla; stir until smooth. Add eggs, one at a time, beating well, then set aside. Sift flour, baking soda and salt together and add to egg mixture, stirring well. Add walnuts and mix well.

Fold mixture into a greased 9-inch-square baking pan. Bake at 325° F. for 25 to 35 minutes. Remove from oven. Sprinkle with bourbon. Cool. Frost with white frosting and Chocolate Glaze. *Yield: 2 dozen*

BUTTERSCOTCH BROWNIES

Boston, Massachusetts

⅞ cup flour, sifted
¼ teaspoon baking powder
¼ teaspoon salt
½ cup butter, softened
¾ cup brown sugar, firmly packed
2 eggs, beaten
1 teaspoon vanilla extract
1 cup walnuts, chopped

Resift flour with baking powder and salt. Cream softened butter and gradually add sugar, blending thoroughly. Beat in eggs and vanilla. Stir in dry ingredients, then fold in chopped walnuts.

Spread batter into a greased 11×7×1½-inch pan. Bake at 350° F. for 25 minutes, or just until fork comes out clean. Remove from oven and mark squares with tip of a knife. Cool on a rack while brownies are still in the pan, then cut into squares. *Yield: 2 dozen*

BUTTERSCOTCH-BLACK WALNUT BROWNIES

Charleston, West Virginia

¾ cup butterscotch morsels
¼ cup butter
1 cup light brown sugar, firmly packed
2 eggs
½ teaspoon vanilla extract
1 teaspoon baking powder
¾ cup flour, sifted
1 cup black walnuts, chopped

In the top of a double boiler, melt butterscotch morsels and butter. Remove from heat; stir in sugar until dissolved. Cool for several minutes. Beat in eggs and vanilla. Sift together baking powder and flour and add to first mixture. Stir in black walnuts.

Spread batter in a well-greased 13×9×2-inch baking pan. Bake at 350° F. for 25 minutes. Remove from oven and cut into squares while still warm. *Yield: 2 dozen*

ZWETCHGENKNODEL
(Bavarian Plum Dumpling)

20 small, fresh ripe blue plums
   (or apricots)
20 large sugar cubes
5 large potatoes, boiled and skinned
2¼ cups unsifted all-purpose flour
1 egg yolk
1 whole egg
2 tablespoons soft butter
⅓ cup sugar
¼ teaspoon salt
   Cinnamon and sugar

Using a sharp knife, slit each plum and remove pit. Place sugar cubes inside each plum. Set aside. Finely grate potatoes into bowl; gradually beat in flour, a little at a time. Beat in egg yolk, whole egg, butter, sugar and salt; beat until dough resembles soft biscuit dough. Place on floured board and shape into a long roll about 2 inches in diameter. Cut into 20 slices, 1 inch thick. Pat each slice into large circle. Shape dough evenly around plum.

Place in deep boiling water and boil, uncovered, for 15 minutes. Remove and drain. Sprinkle with cinnamon and sugar.   *Serves: 6*

APPLE DUMPLINGS WITH GINGER SAUCE

1-crust pastry recipe
5 large tart apples
3 tablespoons hot water
1 cup sugar
¼ cup butter

Roll out pastry to ¼-inch thickness and but into 4-inch squares. Peel, core and slice apples and place in centers of each square. Wet edges of pastry and fold over into triangles. Press edges together with a fork and prick top.

Put water in a large greased baking dish and place dumplings in water. Sprinkle with sugar and dot liberally with butter. Bake at 400° F. for 40 minutes.

Ginger sauce

1 cup sugar
2 tablespoons butter
2 tablespoons flour
3 tablespoons crystallized ginger
¾ cup milk

Combine sugar, butter, flour and ginger; stir in milk. Place over heat and cook until quite thick. Serve sauce over dumplings.   *Serves: 6*

Vienna, Austria
POWIDLTASCHERLIN
(Little Pockets)

1½ cups flour
½ teaspoon salt
1 egg
⅓ cup water
1½ tablespoons melted butter
1 cup jam (any kind)

On a large board, make a well in the center of the flour. Add salt, egg, water and melted butter. Pull flour into well by stirring. Dough will be sticky at first. Knead on lightly floured board for about 15 minutes, or until dough is smooth and elastic. Chill for 30 minutes.

Divide chilled dough into 4 equal portions and roll out each to the size of a cooky sheet. Place 2 dough sheets on 2 cookie sheets and dot the dough with small heaps of jam, about 1 to 2 inches apart. Cover with 2 remaining sheets of dough. Press down firmly between the balls of jam to seal in the filling. Cut out square or triangular shapes with a biscuit cutter. Edges may be crimped to hold in filling more securely.

Drop "pockets" into lightly salted, boiling water. Boil for 10 to 15 minutes (depends on size; "pockets" should float; test one). Lift them out with a perforated ladle and drain well. Serve them with melted butter and sugar.

Serves: 4 to 6

Jerusalem, Israel
ZENAB FRITTERS

¼ cup almonds, crushed
¼ cup raisins, finely chopped
½ cup sugar
½ teaspoon cinnamon
½ teaspoon ground cloves
½ teaspoon freshly grated nutmeg
1 cup flour
½ teaspoon salt
¼ cup sugar
2 tablespoons water
   Oil for frying
2 cups sugar
1 cup water
1 teaspoon lime juice
   Apple juice

For the filling, combine almonds, raisins, ½ cup sugar, cinnamon, cloves and nutmeg thoroughly and set aside.

Combine flour, salt, ¼ cup sugar and 2 tablespoons water and knead into a smooth dough. Roll dough out into a thin layer and cut into 4-inch squares. Place about 1 tablespoon of filling on each square and roll it closed, shaping edges to form "fingers". Fry in oil until golden. Set aside to drain.

To make a syrup, bring 2 cups sugar and 1 cup water to a boil. Add lime juice and continue boiling until mixture thickens. Remove from heat and flavor with apple juice. Dip "fingers" in syrup and serve at once.

Serves: 6

Fort-Lamy, Chad
KAGUE
(Chadian Fritter Cakes)

1 tablespoon fresh or powdered yeast
1 cup milk
2 tablespoons peanut oil
1 cup sugar
4-5 eggs
4 cups white flour
Peanut oil for frying
Granulated or powdered sugar

Soften yeast in ½ cup warm water. Set aside. Scald milk, add peanut oil and sugar. Stir and set aside to cool. Beat eggs into cooled milk mixture. Add 2 cups of the flour and beat until light. Combine diluted yeast and beat again. Blend in remaining flour to make a moderately stiff dough. Knead about 5 minutes until dough is smooth. Place in a greased bowl. Cover and allow to rise in a warm place for about 1 hour. Do not allow dough to rise too much.

Cut into small, round pieces and fry in hot peanut oil until golden. Drain on paper towels. Sprinkle with granulated or powdered sugar.

Serves: 8 to 10

Tejas Verdes, San Sebastian de los Reyes, Spain
SWEET MILK FRITTER CAKES

12 egg yolks
2 quarts milk
1 cup sugar
¼ cup flour
3 eggs, beaten
½ cup olive oil, for frying
Cinnamon
Sugar

Whip egg yolks with milk and sugar. Strain through fine sieve. Place it in a double boiler and stir constantly with a wooden spoon. The sauce will become very thick and creamy. Pour sauce into buttered cake pans. Cool and then chill.

When firm, cut into 2-inch squares. Dip squares in flour and then in beaten eggs. Fry quickly in hot oil until golden. Sprinkle with cinnamon and sugar.

Serves: 6

Addis Ababa, Ethiopia
PINEAPPLE FRITTERS

1 pineapple, sliced
2 tablespoons sugar
½ cup plus 2 tablespoons flour
1 egg, separated
Pinch of salt
½ cup pineapple juice
½ cup milk (or beer)
1 tablespoon butter
Oil for frying
Powdered sugar

Cover sliced pineapple with sugar and let sit for 2 hours. Mix flour, egg yolk, salt, pineapple juice, milk (or beer) and butter into a paste; let this sit for 2 hours. Immediately before using, add one stiffly beaten egg white.

Drain pineapple slices and dredge in the thick paste. Place them in hot oil and fry on both sides. Drain on paper towels and sprinkle with powdered sugar.

Serves: 6

Bahnhofbuffet, Zürich, Switzerland
OEPFELCHÜECHLI
(Apple Fritters with Vanilla Sauce)

> 3 large baking apples, peeled, cored, sliced
> (about 1 inch thick)
> 1 tablespoon kirsch
> 2½ cups sifted white flour
> ¼ cup sugar
> 1 teaspoon salt
> 2 tablespoons oil
> 1 cup dark beer
> ¼ cup cold water
> 2 egg whites
> Vegetable oil (enough to float apple slices
> in 2-inch-deep skillet)
> ½ cup sugar mixed with
> 2 teaspoons cinnamon

Sprinkle apple slices with kirsch. Set aside. Mix flour, sugar, salt, oil, beer and water and let it rest for approximately 1 hour. While batter is resting, prepare vanilla sauce (below).

After fritter batter has rested, beat egg whites until stiff and fold into batter. Heat oil. Dip apple slices in batter and fry them in hot oil until golden brown. Lift out apple slices and shake gently to remove excess oil. Toss in mixture of cinnamon and sugar in a paper bag.

Pass vanilla sauce separately.

Vanilla sauce

> 3 egg yolks
> ¼ cup sugar
> 1 vanilla bean
> 2 cups cold milk

Beat egg yolks until frothy. Add sugar and vanilla bean to cold milk and bring to a boil in a double boiler. Add a quarter of the hot milk to egg yolks, stirring immediately. Return egg mixture to simmering milk, stirring constantly until sauce is thick enough to coat a wooden spoon. Remove vanilla bean. Keep sauce warm. *Serves: 4*

Istanbul, Turkey
LIPS OF THE BEAUTY

> 4¾ cups water
> 2½ cups sugar
> 1 teaspoon lemon juice
> ½ cup butter
> 1½ cups flour
> 1 teaspoon salt
> 2 eggs
> 1 egg yolk
> 1¼ cups vegetable oil

To prepare syrup, place 3 cups of the water in a pan. Add sugar and lemon juice and boil for 15 minutes. Set aside to cool.

Melt butter in another pan. As soon as it begins to change color add remaining water and bring to a boil. Reduce heat to very low, add flour and salt and stir constantly for about 8 minutes. Remove from heat and allow to cool.

When flour mixture has cooled, add eggs one at a time, followed by egg yolk. Beat well. Knead dough and cut into small oval pieces about 2 inches across. Fold these in half so that edges meet, forming "lips."

Over moderate heat, place dough rolls in oil. Increase heat and fry rolls on both sides until brown. Remove and drain.

Place in a dish and pour cold syrup over hot rolls. After 15 minutes, remove rolls from syrup and serve. *Serves: 6 to 8*

Fort Charles Grill, Barbados Hilton, St. Michael, Barbados
BANANA BREAD

1 cup sugar
1 pound (450 grams) ripe bananas
4 eggs
½ cup corn oil
4 cups flour
1 teaspoon baking soda
1 teaspoon ground ginger
½ cup buttermilk
1 teaspoon vanilla extract

Beat sugar and peeled bananas together. Add eggs and mix well. Stir in corn oil. Sift flour, baking soda and ginger together. Add to banana-egg mixture alternately with buttermilk. Stir in vanilla extract.

Pour batter into 2 greased loaf pans and bake at 300° F. for 35 to 45 minutes, or until a cake tester comes out clean. Cool on a rack, then wrap airtight in foil. The flavor improves if bread is allowed to age a day or two.

Yield: 2 loaves

Stockholm, Sweden
CHRISTMAS SAFFRON BREAD

½ teaspoon saffron
1 cup lukewarm light cream
2 cakes compressed yeast
½ cup sugar
½ teaspoon salt
1 egg, beaten
½ cup butter, melted
½ cup raisins
4 cups flour, sifted
Raisins for garnish
2 beaten eggs, for brushing

To keep its color, dry saffron at low temperature in oven for 5 minutes. Crush in a bowl until powdery. Spoon 1 tablespoon of the warm cream over saffron and let stand for a few minutes. Dissolve yeast in remaining cream; add sugar, salt, egg, butter, raisins, dissolved saffron and half of the flour. Beat until well blended. Gradually add remaining flour until dough is smooth, but not too firm.

Turn dough out onto a floured surface and knead for 10 minutes. Place dough in a buttered bowl, turning dough to grease all sides. Cover with a towel and set aside in a warm place to rise until double in bulk—about 1½ hours. Punch down dough; knead lightly.

To shape buns, pinch off small pieces of dough and roll out into 7-inch-long strips. Pinch 2 strips together in center; curl in each end. Garnish with raisins in each curl. Place rolls on buttered baking sheet; cover and let rise for about 45 minutes, or until finger leaves an impression.

Brush rolls with beaten egg. Bake at 400° F. for 10 to 12 minutes. (Saffron bread is a Swedish Christmas sweet bread traditionally served on the thirteenth of December to celebrate the day of St. Lucia.) *Yield: 1½ dozen*

York, England
RICH ROLL DOUGH

1 cake compressed yeast
¼ cup lukewarm water
½ cup sugar
1 teaspoon salt
¾ cup milk, scalded
2 eggs, beaten
1 teaspoon grated lemon rind
4 cups flour, sifted
½ teaspoon ground cardamom (optional)
½ cup butter, melted

Soften yeast in the lukewarm water with ½ teaspoon of the sugar. Let stand 10 minutes. Add remaining sugar and salt to scalded milk, stir and partially cool. Combine softened yeast with cooled milk mixture and stir well. Add eggs, lemon rind and half of the flour (sifted with spice if desired), and beat until smooth. Beat in cooled butter, then add remaining flour and stir thoroughly.

Turn out on lightly floured board, cover and let dough rest 10 minutes. Knead until smooth and soft—about 10 minutes—using not more than ¼ cup additional flour for kneading. Do not add excess flour on board. Place in a greased bowl, being sure all dough is greased. Cover with waxed paper and a clean towel and let rise in a warm place until doubled in bulk—about 2 hours. Dough is then ready to be used for sweet rolls or coffee cakes.

Tel Aviv, Israel
ORANGE-FLAVORED DOUGH

7 ounces (200 grams) margarine
3 cups flour
1 cup orange juice
1 tablespoon lime juice
¼ teaspoon salt

Combine margarine and flour, add remaining ingredients and work into a dough. Knead well. Roll into a ball, cover and refrigerate for several hours.

This dough can be rolled out as a pie crust or filled to make dumplings or rolls.

COCONUT BREAD

1 coconut, grated
   (approximately 1 cup)
2 cups sugar
1½ pounds (675 grams) soft butter
3 eggs
½ teaspoon allspice
1 teaspoon cinnamon
1½ teaspoon vanilla extract
1 teaspoon salt
1 cup milk mixed with
½ cup coconut milk
2 pounds (900 grams) flour
3 teaspoons baking powder

In a large bowl, combine coconut with sugar and cream in butter. Lightly beat eggs and add. Stir in allspice, cinnamon, vanilla, salt and milks. Sift together flour and baking powder and gradually add, mixing thoroughly.

Turn dough into a greased loaf pan and bake at 325° F. for 1¼ hours. Remove from pan at once and cool on a cake rack.   *Serves: 10*

Monrovia, Liberia
PLANTAIN GINGERBREAD

½ cup sugar
1 teaspoon vanilla extract
½ cup water
2 cups half-ripe plantains (or bananas),
   sliced thickly
2⅓ cups flour
½ teaspoon salt
1½ teaspoons baking soda
1 teaspoon ginger
1 teaspoon cinnamon
¼ teaspoon ground cloves
¼ teaspoon nutmeg
⅓ cup butter
1 cup molasses
1 cup sour milk
   or
⅔ cup boiling water
   Whipped cream (optional)

Butter a 9-inch-square baking pan heavily. Make a syrup of sugar, vanilla and ½ cup water. Cook plantains in this syrup lightly. Drain. Slice plantains into coin-size pieces and spread evenly over bottom of buttered pan.

Sift all dry ingredients and spices. Set aside. Put butter and molasses into a saucepan and bring to a boil. Add milk (or water) and dry ingredients alternately. Beat vigorously until smooth.

Pour mixture over plantains in pan. Bake at 350° F. for 50 to 55 minutes. Let stand for 5 minutes. Loosen with spatula. Turn upside down on serving plate. Cut in squares to serve. If desired, top with whipped cream.
          Serves: 8

Hotel Lev, Ljubljana, Yugoslavia

SLOVENIAN STRUKLJU (Boiled Cheese Rolls)

Pastry

1 tablespoon yeast
1 teaspoon sugar
2 cups warm water
1 egg, beaten
¼ teaspoon salt
1½ tablespoons oil
1¼ cups flour

Dissolve yeast and sugar in 2 cups warm water in a large bowl. Stir in egg, salt and oil. Blend in flour until completely mixed. Knead for about 2 minutes. Cover bowl with a damp cloth and set in a warm place to rise for 30 minutes.

Filling

½ cup butter
1 cup sugar
3 eggs
1 teaspoon vanilla extract
3 cups cottage cheese
¼ cup raisins
½ cup sour cream

Cream butter and sugar together. Beat in eggs until mixture is pale and fluffy. Stir in vanilla extract, cottage cheese, raisins and sour cream. Set aside.

Topping

7 tablespoons sugar
3½ tablespoons bread crumbs
3½ tablespoons butter, melted

Thoroughly mix all ingredients. Set aside.

Conclusion

Roll out pastry to ¾-inch thickness. Spread on filling and roll into a log about 4 inches thick and 19 inches long. Wrap log in a cloth, securing ends with string, and boil for 40 minutes in water to cover. Place on a heatproof dish, remove cloth, sprinkle on topping and bake at 450° F. for about 5 minutes, or until topping is brown. Cut into pieces ½-inch thick and serve on wooden plates. *Serves: 10*

Henri Matisse, *The Rumanian Blouse*, 1940

Lancaster, Pennsylvania
SPICE ROLL FILLED WITH APPLE BUTTER

  4 eggs, separated
⅔ cup sifted all-purpose flour
  1 teaspoon baking powder
¼ teaspoon salt
½ teaspoon cinnamon
¼ teaspoon ground cardamom
⅛ teaspoon ground cloves
½ cup granulated sugar
¼ cup light-brown sugar, firmly packed
½ teaspoon vanilla extract
   Confectioners' sugar
  1 12-ounce jar (1¼ cups) apple butter

In large bowl of an electric mixer, let egg whites warm to room temperature—about 1 hour.

Preheat oven to 375° F. Lightly grease a 15½ × 10½ × 1-inch jelly-roll pan. Line bottom, not sides, with waxed paper. Grease bottom lightly. Sift together flour, baking powder, salt, cinnamon, cardamom and cloves; set aside.

At high speed, beat egg whites just until soft peaks form when beaters are slowly raised. Gradually beat in granulated sugar, 2 tablespoons at a time, beating well after each addition. Continue beating until stiff peaks form when beaters are slowly raised.

(continued)

Jean-François Millet, *The Gleaners*

In small bowl of an electric mixer, using same beaters, beat egg yolks at high speed until thick and lemon-colored. Add brown sugar and vanilla, beating until very thick. Using a wire whisk or rubber scraper, gently fold egg-yolk and flour mixtures into egg-white mixture, just until combined (there should be no streaks of egg yolk or flour).

Turn into prepared pan, spreading evenly. Bake at 375° F. for 12 to 15 minures, or just until surface springs back when gently pressed with fingertip. Loosen edges with sharp knife. Invert on dish towel that has been sprinkled with confectioners' sugar. Peel off waxed paper. Trim edges. Roll up from short side, rolling towel inside cake. Let cool on wire rack. Unroll and remove towel. Spread apple butter evenly and reroll. Place, seam side down, on serving platter. Sift confectioners' sugar over top.

Serves: 8

Jean-François Millet, *The Angelus*

Chaim Soutine, *The Pastrycook*, 1922

The Hyatt Regency, Atlanta, Georgia
STRAWBERRY-CHEESE PIE

½ cup uncooked rice
2 cups water, boiling and salted
1½ tablespoons plain gelatin
⅓ cup strawberry juice
8 ounces (225 grams) cream cheese
½ cup sugar
1 pound (450 grams) sliced frozen
    strawberries, thawed and drained
1 cup heavy cream, whipped
1 9-inch baked pie shell

Stir rice into 2 cups of boiling, salted water. Cover and simmer over low heat for 20 minutes. (Equals 1 cup cooked rice.) Soften gelatin in strawberry juice, stir and heat until dissolved. Let cool.

Mix cream cheese and sugar, whip until fluffy. Gradually add cooked rice, cooled gelatin and most of the strawberries. Fold in whipped cream. Pour mixture into baked pie shell and spread evenly with spatula. Garnish with strawberries remaining. Chill before serving.

Serves: 6 to 8

New York City
CREAMY CHERRY-CHEESE PIE

1 8-ounce package (225 grams)
    cream cheese
1⅓ cups condensed milk (15-ounce can)
⅓ cup lemon juice
1 teaspoon vanilla extract
1 9-inch baked pie shell, cold
1 can prepared cherry pie filling

Blend cream cheese until soft; whip until fluffed. Gradually add condensed milk, beating until thoroughly blended. Fold in lemon juice and vanilla. Pour into cold, baked pie shell and chill for 2 to 3 hours.

When chilled, pile on cherry pie filling. Keeps well in refrigerator.

Serves: 8

Newport House, Newport, County Mayo, Ireland
STRAWBERRY OR LOGANBERRY TARTLETS

1 cup flour
  Pinch of salt
½ cup butter
3 tablespoons sugar
1 egg
2 cups fresh strawberries or
    loganberries
  Sugar

Sift flour and salt onto a pastry board. Make a well in the center and add butter. Using fingertips, knead lightly until mixture has consistency of corn meal. Add sugar and egg. Knead very lightly until smooth. Chill at least 1 hour before rolling out.

Line 6 small greased tart pans with pastry and bake at 375° F. until pastry is biscuit color, not brown. Unmold pastry shells and cool on a rack. Lightly crush fruit, fill tarts and sprinkle with sugar.

Serves: 4

STRAWBERRY TARTS

1 whole egg
1 egg yolk
3 tablespoons sugar
3 tablespoons flour
2 tablespoons softened gelatin
1 tablespoon cold water
¾ cup hot milk
2 egg whites, beaten stiff
½ cup heavy cream, whipped
2 tablespoons Jamaican rum
4 baked pastry tart shells
1 quart fresh, ripe strawberries
3 tablespoons red currant jelly
1 tablespoon boiling water

In a saucepan beat 1 whole egg, egg yolk, sugar and flour until mixture is light and fluffy. Soften gelatin in cold water and dissolve in hot milk. Add to egg mixture and cook over moderate heat, stirring constantly until it is hot and thick, but be careful not to let it boil. Stir mixture over cracked ice to cool quickly, then fold in beaten egg whites, whipped cream and rum.

Turn cream mixture into baked tart shells and arrange large strawberries, pyramid style, over cream. Glacé with red currant jelly that has been melted and thinned with boiling water. Keep refrigerated until ready to serve.

Serves: 4

TARTE TATIN
(Apple Tart)

Shortbread dough

1¼ cups flour
½ cup sugar
½ teaspoon salt
⅔ cup butter
1 egg, beaten

Sift dry ingredients together. Cut in butter. Mix in egg, stirring as little as possible.

Apple filling

1 cup sugar
⅔ cup butter
3¼ pounds (1½ kilograms) small Golden Delicious apples

Cook sugar and butter until sugar melts and turns golden. Peel and core apples and cut them in half; arrange them in a buttered, heat-proof mold. Pour caramel over apples and cook gently over a low heat until they are almost tender.

Conclusion

Top mold with shortbread dough and bake at 425° F. for about 20 minutes, or until shortbread is done and lightly browned. To serve, invert mold on a platter that has low sides (in case caramel runs). Serve hot.

Serves: 8

Claude Monet, *Woman with Umbrella on the Right*, 1886

Camille Pissarro, *Kitchen Garden and Trees in Flower*, 1877

Dezaley Restaurant, Zürich, Switzerland

APPLE TART

    1 cup puff pastry dough (see page 174)
    1 tablespoon chopped almonds
    3 cups apples, peeled, cored and sliced
    1 tablespoon sugar
    1 teaspoon cinnamon
    2 tablespoons butter
    1 tablespoon brown sugar

Partially bake pastry shell. Sprinkle almonds on bottom of shell and arrange apple slices. Sprinkle with sugar and cinnamon and dot with butter. Bake at 375° F. for 20 minutes, or until apples are soft. Remove from oven on to rack and sprinkle with brown sugar. Serve lukewarm.

Serves: 6

Amedeo Modigliani, *Little Girl in Blue*

Vancouver, British Columbia
BLUEBERRY TARTS

2 cups fresh blueberries
1 cup sugar
¼ teaspoon lemon juice
1 tablespoon cornstarch
12 baked tart shells
Whipped cream

Rinse 1 cup of the blueberries; set aside to drain. Cook remaining blueberries in 1 cup water for 15 minutes, or until mushy. Strain through a very fine sieve. Add sugar and lemon juice and return to heat; cook for 10 minutes, or until consistency of syrup. Add cornstarch dissolved in 2 tablespoons water; cook until thick, stirring constantly to prevent lumps from forming. Remove from heat and cool slightly.

Fill tart shells with uncooked blueberries. Pour warm glaze carefully over each filled tart; chill. Just before serving, pipe whipped cream around edge of tarts. *Serves: 12*

Francisco Goya, *La Maja vestida* (1797-8)

International Inn, Winnipeg, Manitoba
HOT CHEESE TARTLETTES

Crust

> ½ pound (225 grams) pastry flour
> 6 tablespoons shortening
> 6 tablespoons butter
> 1 egg
> 2 tablespoons water

Sift pastry flour twice. Cut in shortening and butter and mix well to fine crumbs. Add whole egg, then the water gradually until dough can be rolled. Roll dough to ⅛-inch thickness and place in 15 tartlette shells.

Filling

> 2 eggs
> 1 cup sugar
> 1½ pounds (675 grams) cream cheese
> 1 tablespoon marzipan (per tartlette)
> 3 cooked apples
>   Graham-cracker crumbs

Beat eggs and sugar until stiff. Add cream cheese and beat until smooth. Set aside.

For each tartlette shell, make a ball of marzipan. Place it together with 2 wedges of cooked apple in bottom of each shell. Fill tartlettes almost full with cream-cheese mixture. Sprinkle each with fine graham-cracker crumbs. Bake at 350° F. for 25 to 30 minutes. Serve with brandy sauce (below).

Brandy sauce

> 1 cup plus 2 tablespoons milk
> 4 egg yolks
> 6 tablespoons sugar
> 1 teaspoon cornstarch
> 3 teaspoons brandy

In the top of a double boiler bring all but 1 tablespoon milk to near boiling. Mix together egg yolks, sugar, cornstarch and reserved tablespoon milk. When well blended, add to hot milk and cook for a few minutes. Add brandy.   *Serves: 15*

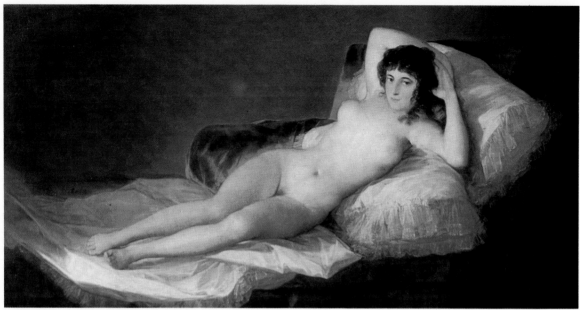

Francisco Goya, *La Maja desnuda* (1797-8)

Tel Aviv, Israel
ORANGE CHEESE TART

Pastry

    2 cups flour
    3 ounces (90 grams) margarine
    ⅓ cup sugar
    1 egg yolk

Combine flour, margarine, sugar and egg yolk and line a greased baking pan with the pastry.

Filling

    1 cup cottage cheese
    7 tablespoons orange juice
    1 tablespoon lime juice
    ⅞ cup plus 1 tablespoon sugar
    2 eggs

Combine cottage cheese, orange juice, lime juice, sugar and eggs. Beat thoroughly.

Spoon into tart shell and bake at 350° F. for 40 minutes, or until golden. Remove from oven and cool. While tart is cooling, prepare topping.

Topping

    1 cup orange juice
    ½ cup sugar
    1 tablespoon orange marmalade
    ½ teaspoon Curaçao brandy
    1 teaspoon coconut, grated
    Orange sections

Put orange juice, sugar, marmalade and brandy in a saucepan. Bring to a boil and cook, stirring constantly, until mixture thickens. Remove from heat, add coconut and spread over the tart. Garnish with orange sections.

Serves: 6

Auguste Renoir, *Torso of a Woman in the Sun,* c. 1875-6

PASTRIES, PIES & TARTS

MARZIPAN-APPLE PIE

Crust

2 cups sifted all-purpose flour
¼ cup sugar
½ cup butter or margarine
1 egg, slightly beaten

In a medium bowl, combine flour and sugar. With pastry blender or 2 knives, cut in butter until mixture resembles coarse cornmeal. Add beaten egg and mix until well blended. Shape dough into a ball then divide in half. Between 2 sheets of waxed paper, roll one half into an 11-inch circle. Peel off top paper; invert pastry into 9-inch pie plate; peel off other sheet of paper. Fit pastry into pie plate and refrigerate.

Marzipan

6 tablespoons sifted all-purpose flour
¼ cup butter or margarine
½ 8-ounce can (110 grams) almond paste
2 eggs

Preheat oven to 375° F. Place flour in medium bowl and cut in butter or margarine until mixture resembles coarse cornmeal. Crumble almond paste and add to flour mixture. Add eggs. Beat with electric mixer until well blended. Set aside.

Apple filling

6 cups thinly sliced pared, cored
apples (about 2 pounds)
⅓ cup dark raisins
2 tablespoons confectioners' sugar
2 tablespoons lemon juice
1 tablespoon golden rum
½ teaspoon cinnamon

In a medium bowl, combine apples, raisins, sugar, lemon juice, rum and cinnamon; mix well.

Conclusion

1 egg beaten

Spread marzipan evenly over bottom of crust-lined pie plate.

Top with apple filling. Roll out remaining dough between 2 sheets of waxed paper to a 10-inch circle. Peel off top paper; invert over filling; peel off other sheet of paper. Press crusts together with fork to seal. Brush beaten eggs over top crust. Bake at 375° F. about 50 minutes, or until crust is golden brown. Cool on wire rack.

Serves: 8

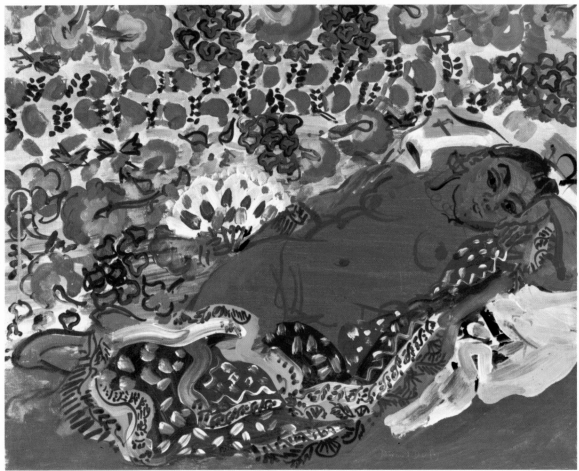

Raoul Dufy, *Indian Woman*, 1928

SINDHI BANANA TWIRLS

Pastry

¾ cup flour
¼ teaspoon salt
¼ cup shortening
2 tablespoons cold water

Sift flour and salt together. Cut in shortening until mixture looks like cornmeal. Add water, a little at a time, using just enough to make dough hold together. Roll out thinly. Cut into eight 6×1-inch strips.

Conclusion

4 bananas
2 tablespoons lemon juice
¼ cup butter, melted
1 tablespoon cinnamon sugar

Peel bananas, cut into halves and dip into lemon juice. Moisten pastry strips with cold water and wrap round bananas in twirls, leaving parts of the bananas exposed. Brush with melted butter and sprinkle with sugar.

Place on baking sheet and bake for 15 minutes, or until crisp. Serve with Chantilly cream or ice cream.
Serves: 8

CROSTOLI

Naples, Italy
PECAN CANNOLI

2 eggs
2 tablespoons sugar
½ cup butter, melted
1½ cups milk
1 tablespoon rum or vanilla
      flavoring (optional)
4 cups flour
   Oil for deep frying
   Powdered sugar

Place eggs in bowl with sugar and mix well. Add melted butter and milk and, if desired, rum or vanilla flavoring. Sift in flour and mix well until you have workable dough. Roll out dough as thin as possible on lightly floured board. Cut into ribbons, 2 inches wide, and fry in hot oil until golden brown.

To crown-shape the Crostoli, use pincers at each end and twist into a circle as they are taken out of oil. Let dry and sprinkle with powdered sugar.   *Serves: 8 to 12*

3 cups flour, sifted
1½ cups sugar
1 teaspoon cinnamon
¼ teaspoon salt
3 tablespoons shortening
2 eggs, well beaten
2 tablespoons white vinegar
2 tablespoons cold water
1 egg white, slightly beaten
   Vegetable oil for deep frying
3 cups ricotta cheese
2 teaspoons vanilla extract
¼ cup cocoa
1 cup toasted pecans, coarsely chopped
   Confectioners' sugar

Sift together flour, ¼ cup of the sugar, cinnamon and salt, then cut in shortening. Stir in eggs, then blend in vinegar and cold water — one tablespoon at a time. Knead dough on a lightly floured board for several minutes, or until smooth. Cover and chill for 30 minutes.

Roll chilled dough to ⅛-inch thickness, then cut into 6×4½-inch oval shapes. Wrap loosely around 6-inch lengths of heavy-duty aluminum foil, rolled to 1-inch diameter. Seal edges of dough by brushing with egg white and pressing together. Deep fry in 360° F. oil until golden brown. Drain on paper towels. Cool slightly and remove foil carefully. Cool completely and store in airtight container until ready to serve.

For filling, combine cheese, vanilla, cocoa and remaining sugar, then beat with electric mixer or in a blender until smooth. Add half of the pecans, then chill.

When ready to serve, fill pastry with cheese filling, then dip the ends in the remaining pecans and dust with confectioners' sugar. Serve immediately.   *Serves: 8 to 10*

Giuseppe Maria Crespi, *Woman Washing Dishes*

Athens, Greece
TIROPETA
(Cheese Pie)

½ pound (225 grams) butter
12 eggs
1 pound (450 grams) ricotta cheese
1 pound goat cheese
1 pound Greek pastry (filo)

Melt half the butter and let cool. Beat eggs until stiff. In a separate bowl mix cheeses with cooled, melted butter and add eggs. Melt remainder of butter and brush both sides of pastry sheets with it. Butter a baking pan large enough for the pastry and 2 inches deep.

Place half of pastry sheets in baking pan and then add cheese mixture. Cover with remaining pastry sheets. Do not cut pastry. Bake at 350° F. for about 30 minutes, or until golden. Cut in squares and serve hot.   *Serves: 16*

Athens, Greece
GALATOBOUREKO

4 cups sugar
1 teaspoon lemon juice
2½ cups boiling water
8 egg yolks
6 cups warm milk
6 tablespoons cornstarch
1 cup very heavy cream
1 tablespoon vanilla extract
1 cup sweet butter, melted
½ pound (225 grams) Greek pastry (filo)

Mix 3½ cups sugar and lemon juice with boiling water and stir until dissolved. Bring to a boil again and simmer for 15 minutes. Set aside to cool. Beat egg yolks and remaining ½ cup of sugar together until mixture is thick and pale in color. Stir in warm milk alternately with cornstarch until mixture nearly reaches the boiling point. Remove from heat and stir in cream and vanilla.

Butter filo sheets generously on both sides and thoroughly butter a suitable baking tray. Place half of the sheets on baking tray. Pour cream mixture over pastry and cover cream with remaining sheets of pastry. With a sharp knife, cut top of pastry into a number of strips.

Preheat oven to 375° F. and place baking tray in it for about 45 minutes, or until pastry is golden. Remove from oven and pour cool syrup over hot galatoboureko. Do not cover dish. Leave to cool; cut into squares before serving.
Serves: 24

RAISIN PASTRY

Crust

    1½ cups flour
    ¼ cup butter
    ¼ cup milk
    ¼ teaspoon salt

Combine flour, butter, milk and salt and work into a smooth dough. Roll out and arrange in a greased baking tin.

Filling

    6 eggs, separated
    ¾ cup sugar
    ½ teaspoon vanilla extract
    1 cup raisins
    ½ cup pine nuts
    2 cups milk

Beat egg yolks until light with half the sugar. Beat egg whites into a foam with remaining sugar. Gently add yolks to whites. Combine vanilla, raisins, pine nuts and milk and mix into egg mixture.

Pour into pastry shell and bake for 1 hour at 350° F.   *Serves: 4*

SYRUP PASTRY

Flan pastry

    ½ cup butter
    2 tablespoons sugar
    1 egg
    1 cup flour
    Water, if needed

Cream together butter and sugar. Mix in egg and flour. Add a little water, a teaspoon at a time, if necessary to make dough hold together. Do not overmix. Gather dough into a ball with a spatula and wrap in waxed paper; let rest in refrigerator at least 30 minutes.

Filling

    2 cups light corn syrup
    ½ cup fine white bread crumbs
    ¼ cup water
    Juice of 1 lemon
    Shredded yellow peel of 1 lemon

Heat syrup and mix in bread crumbs and water. Add lemon juice and shredded peel.

Conclusion

Stand a 8×1-inch greased flan ring on a greased cookie sheet. Roll out pastry quite thin and arrange in flan ring, reserving some for top.

Pour syrup mixture into pastry. Decorate top with strips of pastry. Bake at 350° F. for 30 to 40 minutes. Serve hot with custard sauce or cold with plain or whipped cream.

Serves: 6

APFELSTRUDEL
(Apple Strudel)

2 cups flour
¼ teaspoon salt
1 egg, beaten
⅔ cup water (scant, amount
    depends on flour)
1 tablespoon butter, melted
5 pounds (2¼ kilograms) tart apples,
    peeled, cored and thinly sliced
1 cup raisins
½ cup blanched almonds or
    walnuts, chopped
    Grated peel of ½ lemon
1½ cups sugar
1 cup melted butter for basting
5-10 bitter almonds, blanched and chopped

On a large board, make a well in the center of flour. Add salt, egg, water and melted butter. Pull flour into the well by stirring. Dough will be sticky at first. Knead on lightly floured board for about 15 minutes — until dough is smooth and elastic. Stretch dough and knead again for another 2 minutes. Cover with a china or earthenware bowl which has been well heated with boiling water. Let dough stand for 30 to 45 minutes.

While dough is resting, prepare filling. Mix thoroughly together apples, raisins, almonds (or walnuts), lemon peel and sugar. Also melt basting butter at this time.

Cover large table with a table cloth and dust it heavily with flour. Place dough in the middle of the table, dust with flour and roll out slightly. Dust the back of your hand with flour and, holding the thumb inward, put your hand underneath dough and begin to pull. Lift dough only slightly. If center part is pulled out thin enough, let it drop to the cloth and continue to pull slowly, stretching dough thinly until it covers the table. Let thick ends hang over edges, cutting these off.

Spread filling over dough, leaving an empty stretch of about 1 inch along edges. Pour some melted butter on top of filling. Lift cloth and roll strudel like a jelly roll. Pinch edges closed to seal filling. Brush generously with melted butter. Cut to fit size of pans available. Place strudel, twisted in a crescent shape, on greased baking sheets or in shallow pans, and bake for 30 minutes at 400° F. Bake for another 30 to 35 minutes at 350° F., or until strudel is crisp and brown. Brush with melted butter every 10 minutes during baking. Strudel can be served hot or cold and may be stuffed with other kinds of fruit fillings. *Serves: 10 to 12*

LA FLOGNARDE
(Individual Apple Pastry)

1 apple
2 tablespoons lemon juice
2 eggs
1½ tablespoons sugar
6 tablespoons flour
½ cup milk
1 tablespoon butter
    Powdered sugar

Peel and core apples and cut in thin slices; sprinkle with lemon juice and set aside.

Beat eggs until frothy. Sift sugar and flour together, then sift into eggs; mix gently. Add milk very slowly, mixing thoroughly but gently. Grease a 4-inch springform pan thoroughly with butter. Place in 400° F. oven until hot.

Spread batter in pan and top with apple slices. Bake at 400° F. until crust tests done, only about 10 minutes. (If crust is browning too fast on the edges, reduce heat to 350° F. to finish baking.) Sift powdered sugar over apples and serve immediately. *Serves: 1*

Old Club Restaurant, Alexandria, Virginia
DEEP-DISH APPLE PIE

7 pounds (3.1 kilograms) sliced apples
1 pound (450 grams) brown sugar
1 pound white sugar
3 tablespoons nutmeg
3 teaspoons cinnamon
½ cup plus 2 tablespoons flour
1 tablespoon salt
½ cup apple wine
1 cup apple juice
½ cup butter
3 cups pastry flour
½ cup shortening
½ teaspoon salt
1 cup butter

Place apples in a 15×9×2½-inch pan. Blend sugars, nutmeg, cinnamon, ½ cup plus 2 tablespoons flour, 1 tablespoon salt, apple wine and juice together and pour over apples. Cut ½ cup butter into thin slices and divide evenly over apples.

To make a crust, mix together the pastry flour, shortening, ½ teaspoon salt and 1 cup butter. Shape into a ball and roll out to ½-inch thickness on a lightly floured board. Cover apples and cut 1-inch-long slits evenly in crust. Bake at 425° F. for 1 hour. Lower temperature to 325° F. and continue baking until crust is brown.

Serves: 10

Woodbridge, Virginia
DEEP-DISH CIDER APPLE PIE

1 8-inch unbaked pie shell
6 large cooking apples
¼ cup butter or margarine
¾ cup grated Cheddar cheese
¾ cup flour
½ teaspoon powdered cinnamon
¾ cup brown sugar
⅓ cup butter or margarine for streusel topping

Preheat oven at 450° F. Chill unbaked pie shell. Wash, pare, core and slice apples. Melt ½ cup butter in a saucepan, add apples and stir lightly until each slice is coated. Arrange apples in pie shell. Sprinkle cheese on top. To prepare streusel topping, sift together flour, powdered cinnamon and brown sugar. Cream ⅓ cup butter and work into dry mixture until crumbly. Sprinkle streusel topping over apples.

Bake at 450° F. for 15 minutes, then reduce temperature to 350° F. and bake 15 to 20 minutes longer.

Serves: 6 to 8

Philadelphia, Pennsylvania
SHAKER SUGAR PIE

⅓ cup flour
1 cup brown sugar
1 9-inch unbaked pie shell
2 cups light cream
1 tablespoon vanilla
1 stick (¼ pound, 110 grams) butter
Nutmeg

Thoroughly mix flour and brown sugar and spread evenly on bottom of unbaked pie shell. Add cream and vanilla. Slice stick of butter into 12 to 16 pieces and distribute evenly over top of pie. Sprinkle with nutmeg. Bake pie at 350° F. for 40 to 45 minutes, or until filling is firm.

Serves: 8

APPLE AND BLACKBERRY IN CLOAK

4 apples
½ cup blackberries
½ cup sugar
4 tablespoons butter
  Short pastry
1 egg yolk, beaten
  Light cream or vanilla custard

Peel and core apples. Fill cavities with blackberries mixed with sugar. Top with 1 tablespoon butter for each apple.

Wrap each apple in pastry; bring four corners together at the top (envelope style) and pinch to seal. Brush with beaten egg yolk and bake at 350° F. for 30 minutes, or until crust is golden brown.

Serve with cream or vanilla custard.

Serves: 4

La Paz, Bolivia
EMPANADITAS DE CREMA
(Cream Turnovers)

1 cup milk
¼ cup salt
¼ cup sugar
1 tablespoon butter
6 teaspoons cornstarch
4 teaspoons cold water
2 egg yolks, beaten
1 teaspoon vanilla extract
½ cup chopped walnuts
1 cup flour
2 tablespoons hard butter
1 egg yolk
3 tablespoons milk, hot
  Pinch of salt
  Oil for deep frying

In a sauce pan, combine 1 cup milk, ¼ teaspoon salt, ¼ cup sugar and 1 tablespoon butter and bring to a boil. Dissolve cornstarch in cold water and add to heated mixture. Stirring constantly, allow mixture to thicken. Remove from heat and stir in beaten egg yolks, vanilla and nuts. Return to heat and allow to thicken again, stirring constantly. Set aside to cool.

Place flour in a large mixing bowl and cut in hard butter. Combine egg yolk, 3 tablespoons hot milk and salt; pour into flour mixture. Knead for 10 minutes to make a smooth dough. On a lightly floured board, roll out dough very thin and cut into 4-inch squares. Place a generous spoonful of the filling on each square of dough. Moisten edges with a little water, fold over and pinch together tightly with a fork.

Fry in deep fat at 360° F. until golden brown on both sides.

Yield: 1½ dozen

Whipple House, West Branch, Iowa
HEAVENLY CHOCOLATE PIE

1 8-inch baked pie shell
2 eggs, separated
½ teaspoon vinegar
¼ teaspoon cinnamon
¼ teaspoon salt
½ cup sugar
1 6-ounce package (170 grams)
    semisweet chocolate bits
¼ cup water
1 cup heavy cream
    Sugar
    Cinnamon

Beat together egg whites, vinegar, cinnamon and salt until stiff but not dry. Gradually add sugar and beat until very stiff. Spread over bottom and sides of pie shell. Bake at 325° F. for 15 to 18 minutes and cool.

Melt chocolate bits over hot, not boiling, water. Blend in egg yolks which have been beaten with ¼ cup water. Stir until smooth. Spread 3 tablespoons of the mixture over the cooled meringue. Chill remainder of chocolate mixture. Whip cream until stiff. Add sugar and cinnamon. Spread half of this over the chocolate layer in pie shell. Fold chilled chocolate mixture into remaining whipped cream. Spread over center of pie; chill. *Serves: 6*

Vancouver, British Columbia
CREAMY CHOCOLATE PIE

12 ounces (340 grams) semi-sweet
    chocolate
¼ cup milk
¼ cup sugar
    Pinch salt
4 eggs, separated
1 teaspoon vanilla extract
1 9-inch baked pie shell
    Whipped cream

Combine chocolate, milk, sugar and salt in double boiler. Cook over hot water until mixture is blended. Cool slightly. Add egg yolks, one at a time, beating well after each addition. Blend in vanilla. Beat egg whites until stiff but not dry. Fold into chocolate mixture, blending thoroughly.

Pour into baked pie shell. Let set for 2 to 3 hours. Serve with whipped cream. *Serves: 8*

Richmond, Virginia
RUM CREAM PIE

1 graham-cracker pie shell, baked
6 eggs
1 cup sugar
1 envelope unflavored gelatin
½ cup cold water
1 pint heavy cream
1 tablespoon dark rum
    Bittersweet chocolate

Chill pie shell. Beat eggs until light in color. Beat in sugar. Dissolve gelatin in ½ cup cold water. Place gelatin over low heat and bring to a boil. When gelatin is dissolved, pour over sugar and egg mixture, stirring briskly. Let cool. Whip heavy cream until fairly stiff and flavor with rum. Fold whipped cream into sugar and egg mixture when cool, but not set. Pour into pie shell. Sprinkle generously with bittersweet chocolate. *Serves: 6 to 8*

PRAIRIE DELIGHT
(Chocolate Custard Pie)

4 eggs, separated
½ cup brown sugar, firmly packed
1½ tablespoons cornstarch
1½ cups milk
⅓ cup bourbon
1½ squares (1½ ounces) unsweetened chocolate, melted
½ teaspoon vanilla extract
1 9-inch baked pie shell
1 envelope unflavored gelatin
¼ cup bourbon
¼ teaspoon cream of tartar
½ cup granulated sugar
½ cup heavy cream, whipped
½ square unsweetened chocolate, grated

In a double boiler, beat egg yolks slightly. Add brown sugar and cornstarch and beat until light and fluffy. Gradually stir in milk and ⅓ cup bourbon and cook over hot, not boiling, water, stirring constantly until thickened and smooth. Remove from heat.

Pour 1 cup of the custard mixture into a separate bowl and add 1½ ounces melted chocolate and vanilla; mix well. Cool slightly and pour into pie shell.

Soften gelatin in ¼ cup bourbon. Add remaining custard mixture and stir until gelatin dissolves. Cool slightly. Beat egg whites and cream of tartar until soft peaks form. Gradually add granulated sugar and continue beating until stiff and glossy. Fold egg whites into gelatin-custard mixture. Pour into pie shell on top of chocolate mixture. Chill until firm.

Pipe or spoon whipped cream around edge of pie. Sprinkle with grated chocolate.

Serves: 8

SOUR CREAM PRUNE PIE

2 cups cooked prunes
2 eggs
⅔ cup honey
⅔ cup sour cream
¼ teaspoon salt
1 tablespoon lemon juice
Pastry for 8-inch double-crust pie

Remove pits and cut prunes into large pieces. Beat eggs lightly and blend in honey, sour cream, salt and lemon juice until smooth and creamy. Add prunes.

Pour into pastry-lined 8-inch pie plate. Cover with top crust. Flute edge and prick here and there with fork. Bake at 400° F. for 45 minutes until golden brown.

Serves: 6

San Francisco, California
COINTREAU CHIFFON PIE

  1 envelope gelatin
  ¼ cup cold water
  4 eggs, separated
  ¾ cup sugar
  ⅓ cup orange juice
  ¼ teaspoon salt
  2 tablespoons Cointreau
  2 tablespoons grated orange peel
  1 9-inch pie shell, baked
     Whipped cream (optional)

Soften gelatin in cold water. Beat egg yolks until thick. Beat in ½ cup of the sugar, orange juice and salt. Cook in the top of a double boiler over boiling water, stirring constantly, until thickened. Add Cointreau and orange peel. Cool until mixture begins to stiffen. Beat egg whites; add remaining sugar gradually. Beat until quite stiff. Fold into gelatin mixture.

Spoon into baked pie shell. Chill until firm. Garnish with whipped cream, if desired.

Serves: 8

London
WALNUT PIE SHELL

  1 cup fine graham-cracker crumbs
  ¼ cup granulated sugar
  ¼ cup softened butter
  ½ cup finely chopped California walnuts

Mix well all ingredients. Press into 9-inch pie pan. Chill, or bake at 375° F. for about 7 minutes.

London
EGGNOG-WALNUT PIE

  3 eggs, separated
  ½ cup sugar
  ¼ teaspoon nutmeg
  1½ cups cold milk
  ⅛ teaspoon salt
  1 envelope unflavored gelatin
  ⅓ cup bourbon
  ½ cup heavy cream, whipped
  1 9-inch baked Walnut Pie Shell (above)
     Additional whipped cream (optional)
     Walnut halves (optional)

In top of a double boiler, beat egg yolks slightly. Add ¼ cup of the sugar, nutmeg, 1 cup of the milk and salt; beat well. Cook over hot, not boiling, water, stirring constantly, until mixture thickens and coats a metal spoon. Soften gelatin in remaining ¼ cup cold milk; add and stir until gelatin is dissolved. Cool. Add bourbon. Beat egg whites until soft peaks form. Gradually add remaining ¼ cup sugar and continue beating until stiff and glossy. Fold egg whites and whipped cream into gelatin mixture.

Turn into pie shell. Chill until firm. If desired, garnish with whipped cream and walnut halves.

Serves: 8

Boston, Massachusetts
IRISH WHISKEY PIE

    4 teaspoons unflavored gelatin
    ¼ cup cold water
      Pinch of salt
    ¼ cup milk
    2 squares (2 ounces) unsweetened chocolate
    ¼ cup egg yolks
    ¼ cup plus 2 tablespoons sugar
    ¼ cup egg whites
    2 tablespoons sugar
    ¼ cup sliced almonds
    2 tablespoons Irish whiskey
    1 9-inch baked pie shell
    ¾ cup whipped cream
      Toasted almonds, sliced

Dissolve gelatin in cold water. Cook over double boiler until clear. Mix salt, milk, chocolate, egg yolks and ¼ cup plus 2 tablespoons sugar. Cook until chocolate and sugar are dissolved. Put in a bowl. Add gelatin mixture. Chill over crushed ice until syrupy. Beat egg whites, adding 2 tablespoons sugar gradually. Fold in chocolate mixture to egg whites. Add nuts and whiskey. Fold until smooth.

Pour into baked pie shell. Top with whipped cream and toasted almonds. Keep refrigerated until serving.   *Serves: 6 to 8*

New York City
GRASSHOPPER PIE

    2 cups chocolate wafer crumbs
    ⅓ cup melted butter
    1 tablespoon gelatin
    ½ cup sugar
      Pinch of salt
    ½ cup cold water
    3 eggs, separated
    ¼ cup crème de menthe
    ¼ cup crème de cacao
    1 cup heavy cream, whipped

Combine 1½ cups of the wafer crumbs with butter. Press into bottom and sides of a 9-inch pie pan. Dissolve gelatin, ¼ cup of the sugar and salt in the cold water in the top of a double boiler. Add well-beaten egg yolks and cook over hot water until mixture is thick. Remove from heat and cool. Add crème de menthe and crème de cacao. Congeal until mixture is the consistency of egg whites. Beat egg whites until stiff, adding remaining sugar. Fold into gelatin mixture. Fold in whipped cream.

Pour mixture into prepared, crust-lined pie pan and top with remaining ½ cup of wafer crumbs. Chill well before serving.   *Serves: 8*

Tel Aviv, Israel
ORANGE MERINGUE PIE

Pastry

3 cups flour
7 ounces (200 grams) margarine
6 tablespoons sugar
1½ teaspoons baking powder

Combine flour, margarine, sugar and baking powder. Line a greased and floured baking tin with mixture. Bake at 350° F. until golden. Set aside to cool.

Filling

2 cups orange juice
1 tablespoon lime juice
4 tablespoons sugar
4 tablespoons cornstarch
Water
¼ teaspoon salt
1 teaspoon lemon rind, grated

Bring orange juice, lime juice and sugar to a boil. Add cornstarch, mixed with water, and cook over low heat, stirring constantly, until mixture thickens. Mix in salt and lemon ring. Remove from heat.

Conclusion

3 oranges, divided into sections
3 egg whites
3 tablespoons sugar

Cover prepared crust with orange sections and spoon on orange filling. Top with a meringue of egg whites whipped stiff with sugar. Return to oven and bake until meringue is golden.
Serves: 6

Monrovia, Liberia
COCONUT PIE

¾ cup butter
½ cup sugar
2 eggs
Dash of baking soda
¼ teaspoon nutmeg
1 teaspoon vanilla extract
1 cup milk
1½ cups freshly grated coconut
1 8-inch pie crust, partially baked

Cream butter and sugar well. Beat eggs until frothy and blend with sugar and butter mixture. Add soda, nutmeg, vanilla, milk and coconut.

Pour ingredients into partially baked pie shell. Bake at 350° F. for 40 minutes until golden brown.
Serves: 4 to 6

SQUASH PIE

Pie crust pastry

    3 cups pastry flour
1½ cups shortening
    1 teaspoon salt
    6 tablespoons milk, approximately

Mix flour, shortening and salt well. Add enough milk, a tablespoon at a time, to make pastry hold together. Roll out and line pie plate.

Squash filling

1½ cups cooked squash
    ½ cup light brown sugar
    ½ cup granulated sugar
    1 tablespoon molasses
    ½ teaspoon nutmeg
    ½ teaspoon cinnamon
    ½ teaspoon ginger
    ¼ teaspoon ground cloves
    ½ teaspoon salt
    2 eggs, slightly beaten
    1 cup milk

Mix ingredients in the order given. Pour mixture into lined pie plate and bake at 350° F. for about 1 hour.

Serves: 8

CHESS PIE

    1 tablespoon cornmeal
    ½ cup granulated sugar
    ½ cup brown sugar, firmly packed
    2 tablespoons flour
    3 eggs
    ½ cup butter, melted
    1 tablespoon vanilla extract
    1 tablespoon vinegar
    1 9-inch pie shell, unbaked

Mix together cornmeal, the sugars and flour. Beat eggs well in a mixing bowl and add dry mixture. Add butter and cream thoroughly. Stir in vanilla and vinegar.

Pour into unbaked pie shell and bake at 350° F. for 40 to 45 minutes. *Serves: 8*

TRANSPARENT ANGELA

1½ cups sugar
    ¼ cup butter
    3 eggs, separated
    1 teaspoon flour
    1 cup milk
    1 teaspoon vanilla extract
    1 9-inch pie shell, unbaked

Cream together sugar and butter. Mix in egg yolks, flour, milk and vanilla. Beat well. Beat egg whites until firm; fold gently into mixture.

Pour into unbaked pie crust and bake at 350° F. for 40 minutes. *Serves: 8*

Edinburgh, Scotland
CURRANT TARTS

1½ cups currants
Pastry for 1-crust pie
1 egg
2 teaspoons butter
1 cup brown sugar
1 teaspoon vanilla extract
½ cup chopped walnuts
1 cup whipped cream (optional)

Cover currants with boiling water and set aside. Roll out pastry and cut out twelve 3½ to 4-inch circles to line small muffin cups. Drain currants and mix with remaining ingredients.

Fill pastry shells and bake at 350° F. for 30 minutes. May be served warm or cold with whipped cream topping, if desired.

Yield: 1 dozen

Canterbury, England
ENGLISH DATE TARTS

1 3-ounce package (90 grams)
    cream cheese
½ cup butter
1 cup flour
Pinch of salt
¾ cup brown sugar
½ cup pecans, chopped
½ cup dates, chopped
1 egg
1 teaspoon vanilla extract

Cream together cream cheese and butter. Gradually add in flour and salt to make a pastry. Roll into small balls and press into muffin cups to make pastry shells. Mix remaining ingredients together with fingers and fill shells.

Bake at 350° F. for 15 minutes; reduce heat to 250° F. and bake 10 minutes more.

Yield: 1 dozen

Geneva, Switzerland
MANDARIN ICE CREAM TARTS

¾ cup mandarin orange sections
1 cup sifted flour
¼ cup brown sugar
½ teaspoon salt
⅓ cup salad oil
1½ tablespoons milk
1 teaspoon granulated sugar
¼ cup finely chopped nuts
1 pint coffee ice cream

Drain oranges and set aside. Sift flour, 1 tablespoon of the brown sugar and the salt into a bowl. Combine oil and milk; whip until well blended and pour over flour mixture. Mix with fork, adding 1 teaspoon granulated sugar.

Spoon mixture into eight 3-inch muffin pans. With fingers, press evenly to line sides and bottoms of pans. Combine nuts and remaining brown sugar; sprinkle mixture into tart shells and pat evenly over bottoms and sides. Prick entire surface with a fork. Bake for 12 minutes at 425° F. Cool in pans.

Remove tart shells carefully to serving plates. Fill with scoops of ice cream. Top generously with orange sections. *Yields: 8 tarts*

Paris
BASIC DESSERT CREPES

¾ cup all-purpose flour
1 teaspoon baking powder
4 teaspoons powdered sugar
½ teaspoon salt
1 whole egg, beaten
2 egg yolks, beaten
½ cup milk
½ cup light cream
¼ cup water
1 teaspoon vanilla or cognac (optional)
   Small amount vegetable oil for cooking

Sift together flour, baking powder, powdered sugar and salt in a bowl. Combine beaten whole egg, egg yolks, milk, cream, water and desired flavoring and beat well. Combine this with dry ingredients, using as few strokes as possible. The batter should be thin and slightly bumpy. (Additional milk may be used to maintain thin consistency.)

Choosing a skillet for the desired size of crêpe, heat the skillet and grease lightly with oil. Cooking one crêpe at a time, pour in desired amount of batter and rotate the skillet quickly to spread batter evenly. Cook over moderate heat until crêpe is brown underneath (less than 1 minute for thin crêpes); reverse and cook until just turning brown.

Yield: Approximately ten 6-inch or four 9-inch crêpes

Nancy, France
DESSERT CREPES

3¾ cups sifted flour
1 cup minus 2 tablespoons fine sugar
   Pinch of salt
½ teaspoon vanilla extract
8 whole eggs and 4 yolks
3 cups milk
2-3 tablespoons fresh, thick cream
2-3 tablespoons cognac or other liqueur
2 tablespoons butter, heated to slightly
   nutty color

Combine sifted flour, sugar, salt and vanilla into a bowl. Add 8 whole eggs and 4 yolks, one by one, working batter with a wooden spoon. When batter is properly combined, add milk, cream and cognac to batter. Add heated butter.

Cooking one crêpe at a time, pour desired portion of batter into crêpe suzette pan on stove with moderate heat. (The cooler the pan, the thinner the crêpe.) Cook until light brown on both sides. Let cool.

Yield: Approximately 8 large crêpes

CREPES SUZETTE

Crêpes

> 3 eggs
> 6 tablespoons flour
> 1 cup milk

Beat eggs and flour until smooth. Add milk. Keep batter thin. Cook crêpes paper-thin in a very small frying pan with butter. (The cooler the pan, the thinner the crêpe.) Do not lay crêpes on top of one another and do not fold.

Sauce

> 2 tablespoons kirschwasser
> ¼ cup sweet butter
> ¾ cup sugar
> 2 oranges
>   Peel of 1 lemon
> 1½ tablespoons Cointreau
> 1½ tablespoons Grand Marnier
> 4 tablespoons brandy

Have soufflé pan heated. Place kirschwasser, butter and sugar in pan. Heat well but do not scorch. Cut oranges and lemon peels and squeeze juice into mixture. Mix and let simmer for 10 to 15 minutes, or until sauce becomes a light syrup. Add Cointreau and Grand Marnier.

Place crêpes in sauce and cover with sauce on both sides. Fold each crêpe in half and then in quarters. Lastly pour brandy. Tilt the pan and move rapidly, but gently, back and forth over the flame until liquor ignites. Then level the pan and continue forward and backward movement until flame on crêpes dies. Serve crêpes and pour remainder of sauce over each serving.   *Serves: 6 (2 to 3 small crêpes per serving)*

CREPES SUZETTE ORANGE

Crêpes

> 1 cup sifted all-purpose flour
> ½ teaspoon salt
> 1 tablespoon sugar
> 3 eggs, well beaten
> 2 cups milk
> 2 tablespoons melted butter
> 1 tablespoon cognac

Sift together flour, salt and sugar into a mixing bowl. Combine eggs, milk, melted butter and cognac. Stir in flour mixture. Allow batter to stand 1 hour to improve flavor and texture.

Heat a 6-inch crêpe pan or skillet and brush bottom with melted butter. For each crêpe, pour in 2 tablespoons batter. Spread batter evenly over bottom of pan. Cook, turning once, until nicely browned. Fold crêpes into quarters and keep warm.

Orange sauce

> 2 oranges
> 10 lumps sugar
> ½ cup softened sweet butter
> 1 teaspoon lemon juice
> ¼ cup Grand Marnier
> ¼ cup cognac

Wash oranges well and dry thoroughly. Rub sugar lumps over skin of orange and then crush lumps into chafing dish. Squeeze juice from oranges into chafing dish. (Discard used oranges.) Add butter and lemon juice; cook, stirring constantly, until butter and sugar have melted. Add Grand Marnier and cognac; ignite and quickly pour over crêpes. Serve crêpes flaming.   *Serves: 4 (2 to 3 crêpes per serving)*

Crêpes

⅔ cup flour
1 tablespoon sugar
Pinch of salt
2 whole eggs
2 egg yolks
1¾ cups milk
2 tablespoons melted butter
1 tablespoon rum or cognac

Sift together flour, sugar and salt. Beat together whole eggs and egg yolks and add them to dry ingredients. Add milk and stir mixture until smooth. Add melted butter and rum or cognac. Let batter stand for 2 hours before using.

To cook crêpes, melt just enough butter in a hot pan to coat it thinly. Pour in a thin layer of crêpe batter. Crêpe should set and become brown on underside in about 1 minute. Turn and brown the other side. Set aside crêpes and keep warm.

Camelot sauce

½ cup sugar
1 cup fresh orange juice
¼ cup sweet butter
Peel of orange (include some of the yellow pulp)
Peel of lemon (include some of the yellow pulp)
2 tablespoons Benedictine
2 tablespoons yellow chartreuse
2 tablespoons cognac

Caramelize sugar lightly, making sure it does not burn. Add orange juice, butter and peels. Reduce to about ⅓ of the liquid.

Add crêpes, one by one, turning them over so they are well saturated with sauce. Fold or roll crêpes. Pour over the liqueurs. Ignite and serve quickly with sauce poured over.

Serves: 4 (2 large crêpes per serving)

CREPES VEUVE JOYEUSE
(Lemon Soufflé Crêpes)

12 large basic crêpes (see p. 77)
1 lemon rind
1 cup water
½ cup sugar
1½ tablespoons butter
1 tablespoon flour
½ cup milk
¾ cup sugar
½ teaspoon vanilla extract
3 egg yolks
4 egg whites
¾ cup powdered sugar

Prepare crêpes and keep warm.

Peel the lemon in tiny strips. Blanch for 2 minutes in boiling water and soak in 1 cup water and ½ cup sugar which have been boiled together for 15 minutes. Make a thick white sauce by heating butter, flour, milk, ¾ cup sugar and vanilla together. Remove from heat and beat in egg yolks and soaked lemon rind. Finally, fold in stiffly beaten egg whites.

Place a heaping tablespoon of lemon filling on half of each crêpe; fold over. Place crêpes in oven at 400° F. As the soufflé cooks, crêpes should swell and open. They should be done in about 15 minutes. Remove, sprinkle with the powdered sugar and brown rapidly under broiler. Serve at once.

Serves: 6 (2 crêpes per serving)

LEMON AND LIME CREPES

4 basic crêpes (see p. 77)
4 thin lemon slices
4 thin lime slices
2 tablespoons brandy
2 teaspoons crushed almonds

Prepare lime butter and lemon whipped cream (below).

Melt lime butter in a pan until it begins to bubble. Add crêpes and coat well on both sides. Refold crêpes over lemon and lime slices. Flame with brandy. Remove crêpes to dessert plates, accompanied with a mound of lemon whipped cream on each plate. Spoon sauce left from flaming over crêpes and sprinkle crêpes and lemon whipped cream with almonds.

Lime butter

4 tablespoons unsalted butter
2 teaspoons finely grated lime peel
1 teaspoon lime juice

Soften butter. Work grated peel and juice in. Chill in refrigerator.

Lemon whipped cream

½ cup heavy cream
¼ cup superfine sugar
1 tablespoon finely grated lemon peel
2 teaspoons lemon juice

Whip cream. Mix in sugar and peel. Add lemon juice just before using.

Serves: 2 (2 crêpes per serving)

STUFFED CHOCOLATE CREPES TRIOMPHANTES

¼ cup whipped cream
2 teaspoons pistachio nuts
2 dashes of maraschino liqueur
1 teaspoon sugar
4 small basic crêpes (see p. 77)
1 tablespoon butter
1½ teaspoons superfine sugar
1 teaspoon grated orange rind
   Juice of ½ orange
3 tablespoons cognac
1 tablespoon rum
1 tablespoon Grand Marnier
4 squares (4 ounces) semisweet
   chocolate, melted
2 scoops chocolate ice cream
   Whipped cream for garnish

Mix first 4 ingredients together. Divide among crêpes and roll them up.

In crêpe suzette pan melt butter and 1½ teaspoons superfine sugar. Add orange rind. When sugar is almost brown, add juice of ½ orange. Remove pan from heat. Add cognac, rum and Grand Marnier, then flame.

Place crêpes on warm dessert plates. Add melted chocolate to pan and mix well with liquid remaining there. Pour over crêpes. Place ice cream and whipped cream garnish on either side of the crêpe and serve at once.

Serves: 2

MOCHA CREPES

4 crêpes (see p. 77)
¼ cup butter
¼ cup sugar
1 tablespoon strong mocha-coffee
1 teaspoon crème de cacao
1 teaspoon brandy

Prepare crêpes and keep warm. Finish at the table. Cream butter and sugar and heat in a chafing dish. Add mocha-coffee and crème de cacao. Place prepared crêpes in pan with sauce and flambé brandy.

Serves: 2

Hotel Eisenhut, Rothenburg, West Germany
BANANA CREPES SUCHARD

2 large crêpes (see p. 77)
2 bananas, halved lengthwise
3 tablespoons sweet butter
1 tablespoon rum, warmed
1 teaspoon rum
½ cup chocolate sauce, hot (see p. 184)
½ cup sliced peaches
2 scoops vanilla ice cream

Prepare crêpes and set aside on dessert plates. Sauté banana halves in butter. When golden, flambé with 1 tablespoon rum. When flames have subsided, place 2 banana halves on each crêpe. Add 1 teaspoon rum to hot chocolate sauce and pour over bananas. Garnish with peaches and a scoop of ice cream on each plate.

Serves: 2

Le Grand Veneur, Paris
CREPES SOUFFLES

Crêpes

½ cup milk
½ cup water
4 eggs, separated
1 teaspoon vanilla extract
1 cup flour
¼ cup sugar
Butter

Beat milk, water, egg yolks and vanilla together. Sift flour and sugar. Add liquid to dry ingredients all at once and beat with a wire whisk until batter is smooth. Let batter rest at least 1 hour.

When ready to cook crêpes, beat egg whites until stiff peaks form. Carefully fold egg whites into batter. Cook very thin crêpes on both sides in a buttered crêpe pan or skillet. Fold cooked crêpes into quarters and place in a chafing dish or heatproof serving dish. Keep warm.

Conclusion

2 tablespoons butter
2 tablespoons sugar
1 lemon peel, cut in fine slivers
1 orange peel, cut in fine slivers
¼ cup Cointreau
¼ cup cognac

Melt butter in a small pan. Add sugar and peels and cook gently for 5 minutes, stirring to prevent scorching. Add Cointreau and just heat through.

Pour syrup over crêpes, flame with cognac and serve hot. *Serves: 6 (2 crêpes per serving)*

L'Etoile, San Francisco, California
CREPES SOUFFLES JOYEUSE SOPHIE

6 basic crêpes (see p. 77)
½ pound (225 grams) sweet butter
2½ cups flour
4 cups milk
1 cup plus 6 tablespoons sugar
14 egg yolks
6 tablespoons Grand Marnier
14 egg whites
2 tablespoons sugar
Confectioners' sugar

Prepare crêpes and keep warm.

Melt butter and blend in flour. Add milk and 1 cup plus 6 tablespoons sugar and stir until mixture becomes thick. Blend in egg yolks and Grand Marnier. Whip egg whites, not too stiff, and add 2 tablespoons sugar. Fold egg whites into ingredients.

Put soufflé mixture into each crêpe and fold crêpe in half. Place in oven at 450° F. for 15 minutes. Remove from oven and sprinkle with confectioners' sugar. Serve immediately.

Serves: 6

Bretton's Restaurant, Kansas City, Missouri
CREPES JOEL

Crêpes

    1 cup flour
    2 cups milk
    4 egg yolks
    2 whole eggs
    2 tablespoons sugar
    4 tablespoons melted butter
    2 tablespoons cognac
    2 orange rinds
    1 lemon rind

Stir together flour and milk. Mix egg yolks, whole eggs, sugar, melted butter, cognac and orange and lemon rinds into butter. Let stand about 20 minutes. Strain.

Cook crêpes paper-thin in a small frying pan with small amounts of butter. Do not lay crêpes on top of one another; do not fold them.

Conclusion

    Vanilla ice cream, one scoop per serving
    2 cups chocolate sauce (see p. 184)
    ¼ cup rum
    Sliced almonds

For each serving, place 1 crêpe on plate. On this crêpe place a scoop of ice cream. Place the second crêpe on top of ice cream. At the table, heat chocolate sauce and add rum. Flame and pour sauce over crêpes. Garnish with almonds.

Serves: 10 to 12 (2 thin crêpes per serving)

New York City
THE CREPES OF VENUS WITH GINGER AND ICE CREAM

    1 tablespoon butter
    5 teaspoons fine sugar
      Juice of 1 orange
    1 basic crêpe (see p. 77)
      Ginger
    4 tablespoons mixture of rum,
      Grand Marnier, brandy
    1 scoop ice cream

Melt butter in crêpe suzette pan. Add sugar and cook until it starts to brown. Squeeze juice of 1 orange into pan and mix well.

Place crêpe in pan with sauce. Warm crêpe. Place ginger in pan to heat. Fold crêpe in half and place ginger on crêpe. Fold crêpe in quarters and remove pan from heat. Flame rum-Grand Marnier-brandy mixture and pour over crêpe. Add ice cream on one side of dish.

Serves: 1

CREPES HOTEL VANCOUVER

Crêpes

1¼ cups all-purpose flour
3 eggs
1 cup milk
¼ cup water
½ teaspoon salt
4 tablespoons clarified butter

Beat all ingredients, except butter, together to form a smooth batter. Let rest 1 hour. (Crêpes may be made in advance and stored in refrigerator or frozen.)

Cook thin crêpes individually in small portions of clarified butter. Do not fold crêpes.

Filling

6 tablespoons soft nougat
12 Chinese gooseberries, peeled and sliced
4 tablespoons crème pâtissière
4 egg whites
2 tablespoons sugar
2 tablespoons crushed hazelnuts
1 cup chocolate sauce (see p. 184)
½ cup heavy cream, whipped
2 tablespoons Grand Marnier

Spread ½ tablespoon nougat on each crêpe and place 1 sliced gooseberry on top. Cover with crème pâtissière and roll up.

Beat egg whites until foamy. Add sugar gradually and continue beating to form a stiff meringue. Fold in crushed hazelnuts.

Place crêpes on a buttered silver tray and pipe meringue mixture on top.

Bake at 350° F. for 6 minutes; brown slightly under broiler. Serve with thick chocolate sauce mixed with whipped cream and Grand Marnier.

Serves: 6 (2 crêpes per serving)

CREPES SIR HOLDEN

Crêpes

  ½ cup flour
  ½ teaspoon salt
   1 egg
  ½ cup milk (more if needed)
    Oil for cooking

Sift flour and salt together. Add egg and milk and blend to make a smooth, thin batter. (An electric blender makes excellent crêpe batter in seconds.)

Lightly oil a small skillet and put over medium heat. When pan is hot enough to make drops of water jump, pour in about 3 tablespoons batter and tilt pan to coat evenly. Turn when bubbles form on top side. Set aside and keep warm.

Filling

  1 cup fresh strawberries or raspberries
  1 tablespoon framboise liqueur
  1 tablespoon Cointreau
  1 tablespoon Grand Marnier
  2 tablespoons brandy
  ¼ cup sugar
  2 tablespoons butter
  1 pint vanilla ice cream
      (2 scoops per serving)
  ¼ cup crushed almonds

Wash and sort berries a few hours before using. Drain well and let dry.

To finish filling, place berries in a saucepan or chafing dish. Mix liqueurs and pour over berries; flame. When flames die, lift out berries with a slotted spoon. Sprinkle crêpes with liqueur mixture and set them aside. Return berries to pan and heat gently with sugar and butter, just until sugar is dissolved. Stir carefully to prevent crushing berries. Keep warm.

Place 2 scoops of ice cream on each serving plate and cover with 2 liqueur-flavored crêpes. Spoon warm berry mixture over crêpes and sprinkle with crushed almonds. Serve at once.

Serves: 4 (2 crêpes per serving)

Tel Aviv, Israel
CINNAMON APPLE PANCAKES

- 1 pound (450 grams) apples
- 2 cups flour
- 1 cup cold water
- ½ cup apple juice
- 6 tablespoons sugar
- Peel of 1 lemon, grated
- Pinch of salt
- Oil for frying
- 2 tablespoons margarine
- 2 teaspoons cinnamon

Peel apples, cut into quarters and seed. Cut seeded quarters into small pieces.

Combine flour, water, apple juice, 4 tablespoons of the sugar, grated lemon peel and salt into a smooth batter. Add apples and mix thoroughly.

Spoon batter onto an oiled griddle. Cook pancakes on both sides. Remove from heat, dot with margarine and sprinkle with remaining sugar mixed with cinnamon. Serve at once.

Serves: 4 (3 to 4 pancakes per serving)

Café Royal, Edinburgh
DANISH PANCAKES

Pancakes

- ¼ cup flour
- 1 tablespoon sugar
- 2 eggs
- 1¼ cups milk

Combine all ingredients and make 8 pancakes from the batter.

Set aside and keep warm.

Filling and topping

- 3 egg yolks, beaten
- ½ cup sugar
- 4 teaspoons flour
- ½ teaspoon vanilla extract
- 1¼ cups milk
- 3 tablespoons chopped almonds
- ¼ cup chopped glacé cherries
- ¼ cup apricot jam
- ½ cup brandy
- ½ cup very heavy cream
- 4 whole glacé cherries

For filling, beat egg yolks, sugar, flour and vanilla together in a saucepan. Heat milk just to boiling and add to mixture. Return to stove and cook gently for 2 minutes, stirring constantly. Mix in almonds and chopped glacé cherries.

Divide filling mixture into 8 portions and spread on pancakes; roll. Arrange in serving dish.

Boil apricot jam and brandy together and pour over pancakes. Garnish with cream and whole glacé cherries. *Serves: 4 (2 pancakes per serving)*

Vinograde, Belgrade
PANCAKES "VINOGRADI"

Pancakes

> 2 eggs
> 1½ tablespoons sugar
> 1 tablespoon salt
> ½ cup flour
> 1 cup water

Beat eggs and sugar together. Add salt. Alternately beat in flour and water until completely mixed and smooth. Lightly oil a 6-inch skillet and fry pancakes, using about ¼ cup of batter for each.

Spread filling (below) on each pancake and roll, pressing edges together. Place rolled pancakes in a deep heatproof serving dish. Prepare topping (below) and pour over them.

Bake at 475° F. for about 5 minutes. Watch carefully so that topping does not curdle. Serve immediately.

Filling

> ½ cup chopped nuts (walnuts,
>   filberts, etc.)
> 1½ tablespoons sugar
> 1½ tablespoons raisins
> ¼ cup rum

Mix dry ingredients and sprinkle with rum until mixture is moist and of spreading consistency.

Chateau topping

> 2 egg yolks, beaten
> ½ cup plus 2 tablespoons sugar
> 2 teaspoons vanilla extract
> ½ cup heavy cream, boiling

In a saucepan beat egg yolks and sugar together over low heat until mixture is smooth and creamy. Stir in vanilla. Beat boiling cream in gradually until sauce is as thick as custard.

Serves: 4 (2 pancakes per serving)

Odessa, Soviet Union
BLINCHIKI

> 4 tablespoons flour
> 1 tablespoon sugar
> ½ teaspoon baking powder
> 2 eggs, beaten
>   Milk
> ¼ teaspoon butter for frying
> 8 ounces (225 grams) creamed
>   cottage cheese, drained
> ¾ cup sugar
> 1 teaspoon nutmeg
> 1 teaspoon vanilla extract
>   Sweet butter
>   Sour cream (optional)
>   Jam or fresh fruit (optional)

Sift together flour, 1 tablespoon sugar and baking powder. Add eggs and mix to form a paste. Add just enough milk to make a creamy batter. Place butter in an 8-inch skillet and heat. Cooking one pancake at a time, pour small amount of batter in skillet and thinly coat bottom. Fry only on one side until bubbles form; remove and cool.

To make a filling, combine cottage cheese, ¾ cup sugar, nutmeg and vanilla. Beat well. Place 1 heaping tablespoon cheese filling in center of browned side of pancake. Fold as you would an envelope and roll closed. (May be frozen at this stage.) When ready to serve, sizzle in sweet butter. Serve with sour cream and jam or fresh fruit, if desired. *Serves: 4 (1 pancake per serving)*

TOPFENPALATSCHINKEN
(Pancakes with Cottage Cheese Filling)

Pancakes

2 egg yolks
1 cup milk
1 cup flour
  Pinch of salt
2 egg whites
  Butter for cooking

Beat yolks lightly; add milk, flour and salt. Beat until smooth. Let stand for 1 hour.

Meanwhile, prepare cottage cheese filling (below).

Just before cooking pancakes, beat egg whites until stiff, but not dry, and fold them into batter.

For each pancake, pour a small amount of butter in a 6-inch frying pan and rotate pan to distribute fat evenly. Pour in ¼ cup batter and spread to cover bottom of pan. Lower heat and let pancake cook a few seconds. When the underside is yellow, but not brown, turn and cook the other side until done—about ½ minute. Remove from pan and set aside.

Cottage cheese filling

1 cup cottage cheese
1 tablespoon butter
1 egg yolk
2 tablespoons sugar
2 tablespoons raisins
1 egg white

Press cottage cheese through a fine sieve. Cream butter and beat in egg yolk and sugar. Beat well. Add cottage cheese and raisins. Beat egg white until stiff and fold into cottage cheese mixture. Set aside.

Conclusion

1 tablespoon milk or cream
  Sugar (optional)

Spread cottage cheese filling on each pancake; roll, and place in a shallow, well-greased ovenproof baking dish. Add enough milk or cream to cover bottom of dish and bake at 350° F. for 20 minutes. If desired, the top may be sprinkled with sugar.

Serves: 6 (2 pancakes per serving)

The Tower Hotel, London
CARDINAL WOLSEY COMPOTE

1 pound (450 grams) red cherries, pitted
1 pound red currants
1 pound black currants
1 pound blackberries
4 cups sugar
2 cups water
   Brandy
   Light cream

Carefully wash fruit. In separate saucepans for each fruit, stew in stock syrup of 1 cup sugar and ½ cup water for each fruit. Cook over low heat until fruits are soft but retain their shape. Remove from heat and flavor with brandy to taste.

Arrange fruit in a glass bowl, keeping a quarter of the bowl for each fruit. May be served hot or cold. Serve with cream. *Serves: 10 to 12*

Copenhagen, Denmark
SØDSUPPE
(Cherry Soup)

3 cups sour cherries, pitted
6 cups water
   Grated rind of 1 lemon
2 tablespoons lemon juice
½ cup sugar
1 tablespoon cornstarch
   Whipped cream (optional)

Simmer 2 cups of the cherries in the water with lemon rind until soft and mushy. Purée in blender until smooth. Put purée into a saucepan over low heat and stir in remaining raw cherries, lemon juice and sugar. Stir until well blended. Thicken with cornstarch. Ladle into soup or dessert bowls and when cold, garnish with whipped cream, if desired. *Serves: 6*

Amsterdam Crest Hotel, Amsterdam
STOOFPEREN
(Stewed Pears)

6 firm, ripe pears
2 tablespoons lemon juice
¾ cup sugar
1 cup water
1 cup dry red wine
1 stick cinnamon
1 slice lemon
   Whipped cream (optional)

Peel pears, then cut in half and remove cores. (If small, leave pears whole.) Rub with some of the lemon juice to prevent discoloration. Bring remaining lemon juice, sugar, water, wine and cinnamon stick to a boil. Add pears and simmer about 20 minutes, or until pears are tender but still firm. With a slotted spoon, carefully remove pears to a serving dish, cover and cool. They will be slightly red.

Add lemon slice to the syrup remaining in the saucepan. Cook 5 minutes, or until thickened. Strain and cool. Pour over pears and serve with whipped cream, if desired. Stoofperen may also be served hot. *Serves: 6*

Caprice Restaurant, London
ORANGES ORIENTAL

    4 large or 8 small oranges
1¼ cups sugar
    2 tablespoons corn syrup
    Crushed orange-water ice for garnish

Peel skin finely from oranges, using a potato peeler or sharp knife. Cut skin into matchstick strips to remove bitterness, soak in salt water for 24 hours. Reserve oranges.

After soaking, drain and wash in cold water. Poach peel in a light syrup made with 2 cups water and ¼ cup of the sugar for 15 minutes. Drain peel and finish cooking in a strong syrup made with 2 cups water, ½ cup of the sugar and 2 tablespoons corn syrup. Simmer slowly until peel is slightly brittle and sweet-tasting.

Remove absolutely all white membrane from oranges with a sharp knife. Place in a basin. Make a syrup with 1 cup water, remaining ½ cup sugar and the orange peel and boil gently until syrup is heavy and sticky. Pour over oranges and marinate 3 hours in refrigerator. Serve oranges with the candied peel on top. Garnish with crushed orange-water ice. *Serves: 4*

San Francisco, California
BING CHERRIES AND SOUR CREAM

    2 cups ripe bing cherries, pitted
    1 tablespoon sugar
    1 cup small-size marshmallows
    1 cup sour cream

Reserve several whole cherries for decoration. Slice cherries and combine with sugar. Set aside for sugar to dissolve in juices.

Combine marshmallows, sour cream and cherries and chill for at least an hour before serving. Place in individual serving glasses and top with whole cherries. *Serves: 4 to 6*

Kingston, Jamaica
COCONUT FRUITBALLS

    3 cups assorted fresh fruit
       (strawberries, melon, grapes, etc.)
    1 cup sour cream
½ teaspoon cinnamon
    2 tablespoons maple syrup or
       brown sugar
    1 cup shredded coconut

Wash fruit and, if necessary, peel and cut into 1-inch-size chunks. In a bowl combine sour cream, cinnamon and syrup or brown sugar. Coat fruit pieces in the mixture and then roll in shredded coconut. Chill for 1 hour before serving. Place in a serving bowl with toothpicks for spearing. *Serves: 6 to 8*

Sulo Restaurant, Rizal, Philippines
MANGO WASIWAS

3 ripe mangoes
6 pieces *suman sa ibos* (native rice bar)
2 tablespoons butter
2 tablespoons sugar
1 cup mango nectar
1 cup fresh orange juice
4 pieces lemon peel
1 teaspoon vanilla extract
1 tablespoon caramelized brown sugar
3 teaspoons cornstarch
Dash of salt
1 tablespoon kirsch
1 tablespoon Cointreau
1 tablespoon Grand Marnier
3 tablespoons brandy

Peel fresh mangoes and cut into halves. Flatten the *suman* and shape in proportion to the mango halves to be placed on top of rice bars. Set aside.

Melt butter in a pan and add sugar. Then add the mango nectar, orange juice, lemon peel, vanilla and caramelized sugar. Let boil for a few minutes. Thicken with cornstarch. Add salt. Add the *suman* and the mango halves. Let boil for 2 minutes, then pour in the liqueurs and set aflame with brandy. Serve with the *suman* as base and mango half on top.   *Serves: 6*

Hotel Napoléon, Paris
ANANAS A LA BELLE DE MEAUX
(Pineapple in Kirsch)

1 large pineapple
2 tablespoons kirsch
¼ cup sugar
½ cup heavy cream, whipped
1 cup strawberries
Sponge layer (optional)

Cut pineapple in half, lengthwise. Scoop out fruit, reserving shell, and cut fruit into ½-inch cubes. To this add kirsch and sugar (sweeten to taste — pineapples vary greatly in sweetness). Replace this mixture in pineapple shell, cover with whipped cream and decorate with strawberries; or serve fruit on a sponge-cake base filled with strawberries, if desired.   *Serves: 6*

Hotel Napoléon, Paris
ANANAS BEAU HARNAIS *Back cover photo*

1 pineapple
6 cups fresh raspberries
Spun sugar (optional)

Halve pineapple and hollow out both shells. Carefully wash and drain raspberries; arrange in shells. For a festive and edible decoration on a dessert buffet, arrange filled shells on a block of ice and garnish with spun sugar.

Reindl-Grill, Hotel Partenkirchner-Hof,
Garmisch-Partenkirchen, West Germany

RASPBERRY FLAMBE

2 tablespoons butter
1 teaspoon sugar
1 cup fresh raspberries
¼ cup raspberry brandy
2 scoops vanilla ice cream
1 tablespoon whipped cream
1 teaspoon almonds, roasted and ground

Melt butter in a small skillet. Stir in sugar over low heat until golden brown. Add raspberries and stir well to coat fruit in sugar and butter. Pour in brandy and flambé. Simmer for 5 minutes.

Place ice cream in a parfait glass; pour raspberry sauce over it. Top with whipped cream and sprinkle with almonds.   *Serves: 1*

Gasthaus Gunzenlee, Augsberg-Kissing, West Germany

BANANAS FLAMBE

4 bananas, peeled and halved lengthwise
2 tablespoons butter
1 teaspoon sugar
¼ cup orange juice
1 teaspoon lemon juice
4 tablespoons Escorial green
¼ cup brandy
2 egg yolks
½ cup light cream
4 scoops vanilla ice cream
2 teaspoons chopped pistachios

Fry bananas quickly in hot butter. Sprinkle on sugar; add orange juice and lemon juice. Stir well. Flambé with Escorial. Remove bananas to a hot plate. To the same pan add brandy and boil rapidly. Remove from heat. Beat egg yolks and cream together. Pour into pan and heat over very low heat until sauce begins to thicken. Do not boil.

Arrange bananas in a circle around scoops of ice cream. Pour sauce over all and sprinkle on pistachios.   *Serves: 2*

The Tower Hotel, London

PEACH AND BANANA FLAMBE

1 tablespoon sugar
 Juice of ½ orange
 Juice of 1 lemon
2 bananas, peeled and cut in half,
    lengthwise
2 peaches, peeled and cut in half
1 tablespoon Grand Marnier

Place sugar and orange and lemon juices in a small flambé pan and simmer for 2 minutes. Add bananas and peaches and simmer for a further 2 minutes. Add Grand Marnier, flame and serve.   *Serves: 4*

Brennan's French Restaurant, New Orleans, Louisiana
BANANAS FOSTER

2 tablespoons brown sugar
1 tablespoon butter
1 ripe banana
  Dash of cinnamon
1 tablespoon banana liqueur
1 tablespoon white rum
1 large scoop vanilla ice cream

Melt brown sugar and butter in flat chafing dish. Peel and slice lengthwise the banana and sauté in the sugar and butter until tender. Sprinkle with cinnamon. Pour in banana liqueur and rum over all and flame. Baste with warm liquid until flame burns out. Serve immediately over ice cream. *Serves: 1*

Kingston, Jamaica
BAKED BANANAS WITH VANILLA CREAM

2 green-tipped bananas
⅓ cup apricot preserves
¼ cup orange juice
1 tablespoon gold rum
2 tablespoons flaked coconut
⅓ pint vanilla ice cream, softened

Preheat oven to 375° F. Peel bananas; arrange in a shallow baking dish.

In a small saucepan, heat preserves until melted; remove from heat. Stir in orange juice and rum. Pour over bananas. Sprinkle with coconut.

Bake, uncovered, until bananas are tender and coconut is lightly toasted — about 20 to 25 minutes.

In a medium bowl, with wooden spoon, beat ice cream until smooth and of sauce-like consistency. Serve over hot bananas. *Serves: 2*

Tel Aviv, Israel
FRIED BANANAS

5-6 semi-ripe bananas
  Salt
  Black pepper
  Lime juice
  Margarine
  Brown sugar
  Crushed walnuts

Peel bananas and slice lengthwise. Sprinkle with salt and pepper, to taste, and lime juice. Let stand for 1 hour.

Heat margarine in a pan. Brown bananas carefully, keeping them intact. Remove bananas and sprinkle with brown sugar and crushed walnuts. *Serves: 4*

BAKED QUINCE

Tel Aviv, Israel

**Whole quinces, 1 per person
Margarine
Sugar**

Wash quinces and dry them carefully, removing any outer hairs. Rub with margarine. Bake at 350° F. for 2 hours, or until quinces are tender and reddish brown. Sprinkle with sugar and serve.

Quinces can also be served stuffed (below).

Quince stuffing

**Bread crumbs
Currants
Pine nuts
Lemon juice
Brown sugar**

Prepare and bake quinces as above. After 45 minutes, remove from oven and hollow them out. Combine the pulp with the above ingredients and refill quince shells. Return to oven and continue baking until tender.

Tel Aviv, Israel

DRIED FRUIT STUFFED WITH CREAM CHEESE

**Dried fruit: prunes, dates
   apricots
Ricotta cheese
Grated coconut
Walnut halves**

Wash dried fruit and steam it over hot water in a covered colander for about 15 minutes, or until tender. Set aside to cool.

Make a lengthwise slit in each piece of fruit. Remove the pits and fill with Ricotta cheese sprinkled with coconut.

Garnish each stuffed fruit with a walnut.

Tel Aviv, Israel

QUINCE WITH WINE SAUCE

**5 large quinces
1 cup dry vermouth
5 cloves
½ teaspoon cinnamon
   Juice of 1 lime
3 tablespoons sugar
2 cups water
½ pint vanilla ice cream
2 tablespoons chocolate bits
2 tablespoons coconut, grated**

Cut quinces in half. Remove seeds and discard. Place quinces in a pressure cooker. Add vermouth, cloves, cinnamon, lime juice, sugar and 2 cups water. Cook for 10 minutes.

Transfer to a baking pan and fill quince centers with the liquids remaining in the pressure cooker. Pour remaining liquid into baking pan and bake at 350° F. for 15 minutes.

Chill. Fill centers with ice cream, sprinkle with chocolate bits and coconut and serve at once.

Serves: 5

Jerusalem, Israel
LIME JELLIED GUAVAS

4 large guavas
1 package gelatin, lime-flavored
1 cup hot water
1 cup dry white wine
  Juice of 1 lemon
  Sugar
  Whipped cream

Cut guavas in half and hollow them out. Reserve pulp. Dissolve flavored gelatin in 1 cup hot water. Pour into guava shells. Chill until firm.

Combine reserved guava pulp with wine, lemon juice and sugar to taste. Strain to remove seeds. Pour over filled guava shells. Serve at once with whipped cream.

Serves: 4

Jerusalem, Israel
GUAVAS STUFFED WITH TEHINA

2 pounds (900 grams) guavas
4 tablespoons semi-prepared *tehina*
  (a paste made of crushed sesame
  seeds, available at specialty shops in
  jars and cans in semi-prepared form)
¾ cup water
1½ cups figs, chopped
2 tablespoons coconut, shredded
3 tablespoons pine nuts
  White grapes for garnish

Cut guavas in half and hollow them out. Discard pulp. Mix semi-prepared *tehina* with ¾ cup water. Add figs, coconut and pine nuts. Combine well. Fill guava shells with the resulting mixture. Garnish with white grapes.

Serves: 4

Istanbul, Turkey
MEYVA KOMPOSTOSU
(Fruit Compote)

1½ tablespoons gelatin, unflavored
¼ cup cold water
1½ cups unsweetened grape juice, hot
¾ cup sugar
  Pinch of salt
2 teaspoons lemon juice
½ cup Cointreau
1 cup strawberries
1 cup black cherries, pitted
1 cup melon balls
1 cup sliced peaches
  Whipped cream, flavored with
    Cointreau

Soften gelatin in the cold water. Stir in hot grape juice, sugar and salt; stir until sugar and gelatin are dissolved; cool. Stir in lemon juice and chill until mixture begins to set. Add Cointreau and stir well. Add fruits.

Pour into an oiled mold and chill until completely set. Unmold and serve with flavored whipped cream.

Serves: 8

New Orleans, Louisiana
CHOCOLATE PEARS

2-4 pears
¾ cup sugar
1 tablespoon cornstarch
¼ teaspoon ground cloves
1 teaspoon cinnamon
1 teaspoon nutmeg
2 teaspoons cocoa
1 cup water
1½ tablespoons butter
   Whipped cream (optional)

Cut pears in half, peel and core; set aside. Combine remaining ingredients except butter and whipped cream; simmer until thick and syrupy. Stir in butter. Add pear halves and coat well with syrup. Simmer until pears are soft. Place pears on serving dishes, spoon on remaining syrup and top with whipped cream, if desired.

Serves: 4

New York City
RASPBERRY WINE PEARS

1 cup sugar
¼ cup lemon juice
2 tablespoons butter
2 cups boiling water
8 ripe pears
2 packages (3 cups) frozen raspberries,
   thawed
⅓ cup Port wine
   Sour cream

In a saucepan, combine sugar, lemon juice, butter and boiling water and simmer for 5 minutes. Peel pears, leaving on stems; arrange in a 3-quart casserole. Pour in hot lemon mixture. Bake, covered, at 350° F. for 40 minutes. Cool in liquid; drain.

Sieve raspberries into a large bowl; stir in wine. Lay pears in purée-wine sauce and chill several hours, basting occasionally with sauce. To serve, place one pear on each dessert plate, spoon over sauce and top with sour cream.

Serves: 8

Warsaw, Poland
GRUSZKA PO WARSZAWSKU
(Pears Warsaw)

Punch for soaking cake

1 cup water
1 cup sugar
1 tablespoon grated lemon peel
1 tablespoon grated orange peel
½ cup vodka
½ cup cognac
1 tablespoon rum

Bring water to a boil. Add sugar, lemon and orange peels, vodka, cognac and rum to boiling water. Mix and set aside to cool for 1 to 2 hours.

Apricot sauce

2 cups canned apricots
½ cup sugar
1 tablespoon lemon juice
½ cup Madeira wine

Rub canned apricots through a sieve with a spoon. Add sugar, lemon juice and Madeira. Set aside.

Conclusion

10 pieces sponge cake
10 canned pear halves
1 cup blanched almonds, grated

Soak each portion of sponge cake in punch; then put in a flat glass bowl and place a pear half on each piece of cake. Cover with apricot sauce and sprinkle with grated almonds.

Serves: 4 to 6

Henri Matisse, *Interior with Aubergines*

Tel Aviv, Israel
PRICKLY PEAR PUREE

25-30 prickly pears
4 cups water
Pinch of cloves
1 teaspoon lemon juice
2 tablespoons sugar*
1 teaspoon cornstarch*
2 teaspoons sugar and cinnamon

Boil pears in 4 cups water seasoned with cloves and lemon juice until fruit falls apart. Drain. Put drained pears through a food mill. Measure purée, *adding 2 tablespoons sugar and 1 teaspoon cornstarch, mixed with cold water, for every cup of purée. Transfer to a saucepan and bring mixture to a boil. Boil for 2 minutes, stirring constantly.

Pour into individual dessert dishes and sprinkle with a mixture of sugar and cinnamon. Chill

Serves: 8

Edouard Manet, *A Bar at the Folies-Bergère, c.* 1882

The Tower Hotel, London
POIRES A LA TOWER

4 large whole pears, peeled
2 cups water
1 cup sugar
4 egg yolks
6 tablespoons water
6 tablespoons Marsala wine
Dash of brandy
¼ cup whipped cream
½ cup red currant jam
4 slices sponge cake
2-3 crumbled macaroons

Stew pears gently in 2 cups of water and ½ cup of the sugar. Drain pears, core them and set aside to cool.

Make a cold zabaglione by putting egg yolks, remaining sugar and 6 tablespoons of water in a bowl over hot water. Whisk until mixture is pale and frothy. Stir in Marsala and brandy and beat vigorously until mixture is very thick and light. Remove from heat and continue to whisk until cold. Fold in whipped cream. Chill.

Fill cored pears with currant jam and arrange them on sponge cake slices. Cover with the cold zabaglione and sprinkle crumbled maca-roons over them. *Serves: 4*

Paul Cézanne, *Still-life with Onions*, 1895-1900

Hotel International, Brno, Czechoslovakia
BAKED PEACH "INTERNATIONAL"

  1 tablespoon Curaçao
  5 ladyfingers
  5 peaches, peeled and halved
  ¼ cup sliced bananas
1½ tablespoons toasted, crushed almonds
  1 tablespoon grated dark (bitter)
      chocolate
  1 tablespoon rum
  5 egg whites
  ⅔ cup sugar
  2 egg yolks, beaten
1½ tablespoons grated nuts
  2 teaspoons potato flour
  2 tablespoons sugar

Drop a little Curaçao on the ladyfingers. Place them in a buttered, heatproof dish. Arrange peach halves on top. Mix sliced bananas with almonds and chocolate. Put mixture on peach halves and sprinkle with rum.

Beat egg whites until frothy; gradually add sugar and beat until stiff peaks are formed. Gently fold in egg yolks, nuts and flour. Spoon meringue over peaches. Sprinkle with sugar.

Bake at 400° F. for about 10 minutes, or until meringue is lightly browned. Watch carefully to prevent burning. *Serves: 4*

PFIRSICH KALTSCHALE
(Chilled Peaches in Wine)

4 large ripe peaches, peeled
Granulated sugar
2 cups water
1 cup sugar
¼ cup quick-cooking tapioca
Juice of 2 large lemons
1 tablespoon Rhine or Moselle wine (or another dry white wine)

Thinly slice 2 of the peaches; cover completely with granulated sugar. Mash and strain remaining 2 peaches; pour over sliced peaches. Combine water, 1 cup sugar, tapioca and lemon juice and boil for 5 minutes. Stir in wine. Pour over peaches. Chill before serving.

Serves: 4

Edouard Manet, *Le Déjeuner sur l'Herbe*, 1863

Auguste Renoir, *Young Girl Bathing,* 1892

Auguste Renoir, *Young Girl Combing Her Hair,* 1894

London Tavern, London Hilton Hotel, London
REAL PEACH MELBA

4 peaches, fresh
2 cups milk
4 eggs, slightly beaten
1 cup sugar
1 teaspoon vanilla extract
1¼ cups heavy cream
½ cup raspberries, puréed

Scald peaches briefly in hot water; peel and split into halves.

Make an egg custard by scalding the milk and then adding beaten eggs. Add sugar and vanilla. Remove custard from stove, cool and place in the refrigerator to chill thoroughly. When chilled, fold cream into custard and store mixture in the coldest part of the refrigerator.

When custard is very cold and thick, place large spoonfuls in the bottom of 4 dessert dishes or champagne glasses. Place 2 peach halves on either side. Top with unsweetened raspberry purée.

Serves: 4

Murillo, *The Melon Eaters*

London
SHERRIED FRUIT CUP

½ cup melon balls (cantaloupe or Persian)
½ cup halved fresh strawberries
½ cup fresh blueberries
2 tablespoons sugar
2 tablespoons sherry or orange juice
½ tablespoon brandy or cognac (optional)
2 fresh mint sprigs

In a large bowl, combine melon balls, strawberries, blueberries, sugar, sherry and brandy, if, desired. Refrigerate, covered, until well chilled — several hours or overnight.

Before serving, stir once and spoon into 2 dessert dishes. Garnish with mint sprigs.

Serves: 2 generously

Gabriel Metsu, *Woman Peeling Apples*

Fernand Léger, *Still-life with Three Fruits*, 1954

Jerusalem, Israel

CREAMY APPLE AND PEAR ROLL

2 cups cottage cheese
1 cup plain yogurt
2 apples, peeled, cored and mashed
2 pears, peeled, cored and mashed
½ teaspoon cinnamon
¼ teaspoon lemon peel, grated
2 teaspoons sugar
½ teaspoon almond extract
  Walnut halves
  Orange slices
  Raisins

Combine cottage cheese and yogurt in a mixing bowl. Add mashed apples and pears together with cinnamon, lemon peel, sugar and almond extract, blending thoroughly.

Shape cheese mixture into the form of a roll. Garnish with walnut halves. Transfer to a serving platter and surround with orange slices sprinkled with raisins.

Serves: 4

Luchow's, New York City
KASTANIEN IN APFELN
(Chestnuts with Apples)

4 cooking apples, peeled, cored and
    cut in eighths
  Juice and rind of 1 large lemon
½ cup water
¼ cup sugar
1 can (11 ounces) chestnuts,
    drained and cut in half
2 tablespoons white wine (optional)
  Whipped cream (optional)

Combine apples, lemon juice and rind, water and sugar in a medium-size saucepan; simmer gently about 7 minutes, or until apples are nearly tender and water becomes syrupy. Stir in chestnuts and wine to taste, if desired. Chill.

Before serving, top with whipped cream.

Serves: 6 to 8

Jerusalem, Israel
CINNAMON JELLIED APPLES

6 large tart apples
6 teaspoons sugar
2 teaspoons raisins
1 teaspoon cinnamon
1 package gelatin, black
    cherry-flavored
2 cups hot water
  Fresh cherries for garnish

Core apples. Combine sugar, raisins and cinnamon and fill the core holes. Place apples in a greased baking dish and bake at 350° F. for about 45 minutes. Remove from oven and set aside to cool.

Dissolve flavored gelatin in 2 cups hot water. Set aside to cool.

Place baked apples in individual dessert bowls. Pour gelatin in. Chill until firm. Garnish with cherries.

Serves: 6

Jerusalem, Israel
APPLES IN WINE

½ cup currants
1 pound (450 grams) apples
¾ cup water
¾ cup sugar
⅛ teaspoon salt
2 tablespoons cornstarch
½ cup rosé wine
3 egg yolks
1 teaspoon vanilla extract
  Pinch of nutmeg
  Sweet seedless grapes

Soak currants in water to cover to ½ hour. Drain. Peel, core and quarter apples. Cook them in ¾ cup water with the sugar and salt in a saucepan until tender. Put through a food mill and return to the saucepan. Make a paste of the cornstarch and wine. Stir this into puréed apples and cook over low heat, stirring constantly with a wooden spoon, for 10 minutes. Set aside to cool.

Beat in egg yolks, vanilla and nutmeg. Stir until mixture is smooth. Spoon into dessert bowls and garnish with grapes.

Serves: 6

COUPE ST. JACQUES

Fresh fruit compote
Kirschwasser
1 small scoop orange sherbet
1 small scoop lemon sherbet
1 small scoop raspberry sherbet
Fresh strawberries

Marinate any desired combination of fresh fruit in kirschwasser. Fill in champagne glass. On top put 1 small scoop each of orange sherbet, lemon sherbet and raspberry sherbet. Decorate with fresh strawberries. Sprinkle few drops of kirschwasser over it and serve.   *Serves: 1*

LOTUS ICE CREAM

2 cups almonds
6 cups sugar
4 quarts heavy cream
   Grated rinds of 10 lemons
2 tablespoons almond flavoring
2 teaspoons vanilla extract
2 cups lemon juice

Brown almonds in oven — then chop fine. Stir sugar into cream. Add almonds, grated lemon rind, almond flavoring and vanilla. Stir in lemon juice and freeze.   *Yield: 1½ quarts*

COUPE "THE PENINSULA"

2 egg yolks
2 teaspoons granulated sugar
4 tablespoons Marsala wine
2 tablespoons white wine
2 scoops vanilla ice cream
2 tablespoons Jamaican rum

To make a sabayon, beat egg yolks and sugar together in a copper bowl. Blend Marsala and white wine into mixture and heat gently over hot water. Keep beating until mixture becomes a creamy, white foam.

Put a scoop of vanilla ice cream into each goblet. Add a few drops of Jamaican rum. Pour hot sabayon over and serve immediately.   *Serves: 2*

ICE CREAM TORTONI

½ pint vanilla ice cream
6 macaroons, (1½ inches in diameter)
½ pressurized can whipped topping
¼ cup chopped maraschino cherries
½ teaspoon almond extract

Place 2 fluted paper baking cups in each of 12 muffin-pan cups. Soften ice cream quickly with electric mixer or with spoon in a bowl. Set aside. Whirl macaroons in blender until crumbs form or pull apart with fingers to form crumbs.

To softened ice cream, add ⅔ cup macaroon crumbs, ½ cup of the whipped topping, cherries and almond extract. Spoon tortoni mixture into cups; sprinkle tops with remaining crumbs. Decorate with remaining whipped topping. Freeze until firm.   *Serves: 6 to 8*

Auguste Renoir, *The Swing*, 1876

Edouard Manet, *Music in the Tuileries Gardens*, 1861

Amsterdam Crest Hotel, Amsterdam
BLUEBFRRY PARFAIT "CREST"

8 egg yolks
1 cup plus 1 tablespoon sugar syrup
5 tablespoons blueberry liqueur
3½ ounces (100 grams) blueberries
1 cup whipped cream

Mix together egg yolks and 1 cup of the sugar syrup in a bowl placed in lukewarm water until stiff; cool. Add 2 tablespoons of the blueberry liqueur, blueberries and ½ cup whipped cream. Mix airily. Pour mixture into a freezer mold and place in freezer for at least 3 hours prior to serving.

Just before serving, remove from mold, place on a serving dish and garnish with remaining whipped cream flavored with remaining blueberry liqueur and 1 tablespoon sugar syrup.

Serves: 8

Mount Soche Hotel, Blantyre-Limbe, Malawi
PARFAIT SAINT TROPEZ

2 layers sponge cake
1 pint chocolate ice cream
1 pint vanilla ice cream
¼ cup brandy
6 ounces (170 grams) bitter chocolate
Whipped cream

In 4 individual (2½-inch diameter) molds or a 1½-quart soufflé dish, place: a thin slice of sponge cake, cut to fit the mold; the chocolate ice cream, slightly softened to spread; another layer of sponge cake; the vanilla ice cream and finally a double-thick layer of cake. Sprinkle the last layer of cake with brandy. Wrap well in foil and freeze very firm — overnight, if possible.

To serve, melt chocolate and let cool to spreading consistency. Unmold frozen ice-cream cake and frost with chocolate quickly. Top with whipped cream.

Serves: 4

Edouard Manet, *The Balcony*, 1868-9

Nicolas Lancret, *The Game of Pied-de-boeuf, c. 1738*

Basel, Switzerland
STRAWBERRIES QUORUM

2 cups fresh strawberries,
   stemmed, washed and quartered
4 tablespoons kirschwasser
2 teaspoons butter
2 teaspoons sugar
  Juice of 1 orange
  Peel of 1 orange
  Peel of 1 lemon
3 tablespoons Cointreau
1½ tablespoons cognac
1½ tablespoons rum
  Vanilla ice cream

Soak quartered strawberries in kirschwasser overnight.

Melt butter in chafing dish. Add sugar and cook until lightly browned. Add orange juice and orange and lemon peels. Add strawberries with kirschwasser and Cointreau and heat thoroughly. Add cognac and rum and set aflame before serving over vanilla ice cream. Be sure to ladle all juices from pan over ice cream.

Serves: 4

Elisabeth-Louise Vigée-Lebrun, *Portrait of Madame Vigée-Lebrun and her Daughter, c. 1789*

Giambelli Restaurant, New York City

STRAWBERRIES A LA GIAMBELLI

2 tablespoons granulated sugar
¼ orange, rind only
½ lemon, rind only
1 tablespoon lemon juice
4 tablespoons orange juice
1 cup fresh, ripe strawberries, stemmed and washed
1 banana (ripe but firm), peeled and sliced
2 tablespoons Grand Marnier
1 tablespoon orange Curaçao or Triple Sec
2 tablespoons fine sugar
2 tablespoons brandy
Vanilla ice cream
Whipped cream

In a saucepan over low heat, melt granulated sugar with orange and lemon rinds until sugar is blond-brownish in color (caramelled). Add the fruit juices and stir until they are caramelled with sugar. Add fresh fruits and cook 5 to 6 minutes until juice penetrates them (watch that the fruits do not burn). Add Grand Marnier and Curaçao and cook a few minutes more. Sprinkle with fine sugar. Add brandy and slide pan around to enable brandy to flame.

Serve over vanilla ice cream and top with whipped cream. *Serves: 2*

Eugene-Louis Boudin, *Woman in White on the Beach at Trouville*

Geneva, Switzerland
PINEAPPLE-PEACH MELBA

1 pint vanilla ice cream, softened
½ 8-ounce can (110 grams) crushed pineapple, well drained
2 small fresh peaches
2 tablespoons brandy
½ 10-ounce package, (150 grams) frozen raspberries, thawed, undrained

In chilled large bowl of electric mixer, at low speed, beat ice cream just until mushy. Quickly stir in pineapple until well combined with ice cream. Turn mixture into a small baking pan; cover with foil. Freeze mixture until firm — several hours or overnight.

Wash peaches; peel. Cut peaches in half; remove pits. Place peach halves in medium-sized bowl; sprinkle with brandy. Press raspberries and juice through a sieve to make a purée. Pour over peaches. Refrigerate, covered, for several hours or overnight.

With slotted spoon, remove peach halves to individual serving plates. Place a scoop of pineapple ice cream in center of each peach half; spoon raspberry sauce over top.

Serves: 2 generously

Atlanta, Georgia
PEACH-BRANDY ICE CREAM

4 fresh peaches, peeled and sliced
   Sugar to taste
1 pint peach or rich vanilla ice cream,
   softened
¼ cup peach or apricot brandy

Combine peaches and sugar to taste and lightly purée in blender. Mix the peaches with ice cream and add brandy. Spoon into parfait glasses and freeze.   *Serves: 4*

New York City
CHERRIES JUBILEE

1 16-ounce can (450 grams) dark sweet
   cherries, pitted (in syrup)
2 tablespoons sugar
   Pinch of salt
2 teaspoons cornstarch
½ cup rum
1 quart rich vanilla ice cream

Drain cherries, reserving syrup. Add enough water to syrup to make 1 cup. In a saucepan combine syrup with sugar, salt and cornstarch. Cook over low heat until mixture slightly thickens. Add cherries.

Prepare individual servings of ice cream. Transfer cherry mixture to chafing dish and heat. Add rum and ignite. While still lit, spoon Cherries Jubilee over ice cream.

Serves: 4 to 6

Zürich, Switzerland
SPUMONI

1 cup milk
3 egg yolks, slightly beaten
   Pinch of salt
½ cup sugar
½ teaspoon vanilla extract
¾ cup heavy cream, whipped
6 maraschino cherries, finely chopped
2 tablespoons candied orange peel,
   finely chopped
1 tablespoon blanched almonds,
   finely slivered
4 teaspoons brandy

In the top of a double boiler, combine milk, egg yolks, salt and ⅓ cup of the sugar. Stir constantly over simmering water until mixture thickens and coats a metal spoon. Remove from heat, cool and add vanilla. Freeze until almost firm.

Carefully line the insides of a 1-quart mold with the frozen mixture. Combine remaining sugar with whipped cream and add fruits, almonds and brandy. Fill center of lined mold, cover and freeze until very firm.

To serve, unmold on serving platter and slice.

Serves: 4

VANILLA ICE-CREAM FRITTERS WITH HOT RASPBERRIES

1 cup fresh raspberries
2 tablespoons sugar
¼ cup raspberry brandy
½ cup vanilla ice cream
2 cups ladyfingers, crumbled
1 egg white, beaten
½ cup almonds, slivered
½ cup nuts, ground
½ cup oil for frying

Soak raspberries in sugar and brandy and set aside. Blend ice cream and crumbled ladyfingers until mixture is very firm. Form into balls. Chill.

Dip balls into egg white, roll in almonds and then in nuts. Drop into very hot oil, turning rapidly, for no more than 30 seconds. Have raspberry sauce heating and serve hot over ice-cream fritters.

Serves: 2

MOZARTKUGEL

1 cup raspberries
2 tablespoons sugar
¼ cup red wine
2 scoops chocolate ice cream
2 tablespoons shaved
**   semisweet chocolate**
Rum
2 tablespoons whipped cream

Boil raspberries with sugar and red wine until mushy. Cool. Pour into parfait glasses. Roll scoops of ice cream in shaved chocolate. Place on top of raspberries. Pour a dash of rum in each glass. Garnish with whipped cream.

Serves: 2

That Steak Joynt, Chicago, Illinois
STEAK JOYNT FLAMING HOT FUDGE SUNDAE

    3 cups hot fudge sauce (below)
    2 tablespoons butter
    6 tablespoons Vandermint liqueur
    6 tablespoons brandy
    1 pint rich vanilla ice cream

Place hot fudge in buttered flat chafing dish over heat and cook until it sizzles. Add Vandermint and brandy. Set aflame and immediately serve over scoops of rich vanilla ice cream in champagne glasses.

Hot fudge sauce

    3½ cups sugar
    ¼ cup corn syrup
    1⅔ cups milk
    4 ounces (110 grams) bitter chocolate
    ½ cup butter
    ½ teaspoon vanilla extract

Cook sugar, syrup, milk and chocolate until mixture forms a very soft ball in cold water (235° F. on a candy thermometer). Remove from heat and add butter. (If sweet butter is used, add salt to taste.) Cool without stirring until lukewarm. Add vanilla and stir in well. Stores well in refrigerator.   *Serves: 6*

Restaurant de la Mere Guy, Lyon, France
MARJOLAINE GLACE AU CHOCOLAT

    2 cups slivered almonds
    2 cups sugar
    2 cups melted butter
    4 whole eggs
    4 egg yolks
    1 cup chocolate ice cream
    2 tablespoons vanilla sugar

Crush almonds in a pestle, remove to a bowl and add sugar, melted butter, whole eggs and egg yolks, to make a rather compact batter. Spread it on a pastry board and roll out to 1 inch in thickness. Bake at 220° F. until dry and light brown — about 1½ hours. Let cool.

Cut almond pastry in half. Place one layer on top of the other with chocolate ice cream in between. Store in freezer until 10 minutes before serving. Sprinkle with vanilla sugar and serve.   *Serves: 4*

Belle Avenue, Göteborg, Sweden
BLACK CURRANT SHERBET BELLE AVENUE

4 cups water
4 cups sugar
Juice of 4 lemons
4 lemon peels
¼ cup black currant juice
2 cups light cream
Nut Ring (below)
1 cup rum

Bring the water, sugar, lemon juice and lemon peels to a boil. Strain through a cloth and flavor with black currant juice. Put in freezer.

When sherbet is half frozen, stir in cream.

Serve frozen sherbet in Nut Ring soaked with rum.

Nut Ring

2 tablespoons butter
¼ cup sugar
2 eggs, separated
2 tablespoons grated nougat
3 tablespoons grated almonds

Whip butter, add 2 tablespoons of the sugar and the egg yolks. Combine the nougat and almonds and mix in. Whip egg whites with remaining sugar. Fold into egg-yolk mixture and pour into buttered and floured ring-shaped mold.

Bake at 350° F. for about 25 minutes.

Serves: 4

Addis Ababa, Ethiopia
KISSEL
(Frozen Orange Dessert)

2 pounds (900 grams) oranges
(or 4 cups orange, pineapple or
other fruit juice)
1¾ cups sugar
2 cups water
½ cup *maizena* (cornstarch)
½ cup cold water

Squeeze oranges (you will need at least 3½ cups of juice). Pour juice into a pot; add sugar and 2 cups water. Bring to a boil. Dilute the *maizena* in ½ cup cold water and stir it into the boiling orange juice. Reduce heat and cook, stirring with a spatula, until the mixture is oily and transparent — several minutes. Remove from heat and cool slightly.

Pour into a chilled bowl or lightly greased mold. Freeze for 2 to 3 hours. Unmold and serve.
Serves: 6

Copenhagen, Denmark
APPELSINFROMAGE
(Orange Snow)

10 eggs, separated
1½ cups sugar
1 envelope unflavored gelatin
¼ cup cold water
Juice of 6 oranges, strained (1½ cups)
Whipped cream

Beat egg yolks and sugar until lemon colored. Soak gelatin in cold water, then dissolve over hot water. Add gelatin and orange juice to egg-yolk mixture. Cool in refrigerator until just beginning to set. Beat egg whites until stiff; fold gently but completely into chilled mixture. Refrigerate until completely set. Serve topped with whipped cream.
Serves: 8 to 10

Rôtisserie des Cordeliers, Nancy, France
SORBET VIEUX KIRSCH

Sherbet

    1 cup brandied cherries
    ¼ cup superfine sugar
    2 tablespoons lemon juice
    1 egg white
    1 tablespoon kirsch

Reserve 2 whole cherries for decoration. Purée remaining cherries and add sugar and lemon juice; mix until sugar is completely dissolved. Beat egg white until if forms soft peaks. Fold in cherry mixture and kirsch. Turn into ice tray or freezer dish and freeze until firm. Stir several times during freezing to break up ice crystals.

Syrup

    ½ cup kirsch
    ¼ cup water
    2 cups sugar

Boil kirsch, water and sugar together until syrup forms a very soft ball in cold water (235° F. on a candy thermometer).

Conclusion

    Superfine sugar

To serve, place 2 scoops of sherbet in a dessert dish. Cover with syrup and decorate with a reserved brandied cherry rolled in superfine sugar.   *Serves: 2*

Ft. Lauderdale, Florida
AVOCADO SHERBET

    1 cup sugar
    1 cup water
    1 cup sieved avocado
    Juice of 2 lemons (½ cup)
    1 cup pineapple juice
    2 egg whites
    4 tablespoons sugar

In a saucepan, combine 1 cup sugar and the water and bring to a boil. Stir until sugar is completely dissolved; cool. Add avocado and fruit juices and mix thoroughly. Place in refrigerator tray and freeze until mushy.

Beat egg whites until stiff; gradually beat in 4 tablespoons sugar until stiff peaks form. Fold into mixture and freeze until firm.   *Serves: 8*

The Tower Hotel, London
LEMON SORBET

    1 cup sugar
    2 cups boiling water
    2 cups sweet wine
    Juice of 2 lemons
    Juice of 1 orange
    3 egg whites, beaten stiff and shiny
    1 cup whipped cream

Dissolve sugar in the boiling water, boil for 5 minutes, strain and cool. Add wine, fruit juices and beaten egg whites to the syrup.

Pour mixture into an ice-cream freezer packed with crushed ice. Set at medium speed, scraping sides so that it does not stick or form ice particles. When almost frozen, fold in whippd cream. Turn into an airtight plastic bowl and store in the freezer.

To serve, let soften a little as very hard sorbet has an unpleasant texture.   *Serves: 4*

Kingston, Jamaica
FRESH-COCONUT SHERBET

1 coconut
2 cups milk
½ cup boiling water
½ cup granulated sugar
1 tablespoon light corn syrup
⅔ cup water
2 egg whites
¼ teaspoon salt
1 cup heavy cream, whipped
  Sliced mango (optional)

Crack coconut shell in halves; remove meat from shell. Pare brown skin from coconut pieces; cut coconut into small pieces. Put coconut pieces and milk (half at a time) in electric blender container; cover. Blend at high speed until coconut is finely grated. Turn into a large bowl. Pour boiling water over grated coconut mixture. Let stand 30 minutes.

Strain through double thickness of cheesecloth, pressing out enough coconut milk to measure 2⅓ cups. Measure 1 cup of the grated coconut and add to coconut milk; set aside. Reserve remaining grated coconut for garnish.

In a medium-sized saucepan, combine sugar, corn syrup and ⅔ cup water. Cook over medium heat, stirring, until sugar is dissolved. Bring to a boil, without stirring; cook to 238° F. on a candy thermometer—until a little of the mixture forms a soft ball in cold water.

In large bowl of electric mixer, beat egg whites with salt at high speed until stiff peaks from when beater is slowly raised.

With mixer at high speed, gradually pour hot syrup in a thin stream over egg whites. Continue beating at high speed until mixture is thick and shiny.

With rubber scraper or wire whisk, fold coconut-milk mixture and half of the whipped cream into egg-white mixture; blend well.

Turn into ice-cube trays; keep in freezer until mushy — about 1 hour.

Turn into a large bowl; beat until just smooth. Return to ice-cube trays; keep in freezer until mushy — about ½ hour. Beat mixture again just until smooth; then freeze sherbet until firm.

To serve: Scoop sherbet into small balls. If desired, heap in coconut shells and garnish with reserved grated coconut and sliced mango. Top with remaining whipped cream.

Serves: 4

Charleston, South Carolina
GINGER PUDDING

½ cup rice, uncooked
5 cups cold milk
½ cup sugar
  Pinch of salt
2 teaspoons vanilla extract
½ cup preserved ginger and syrup
2 cups heavy cream, whipped

In a 2-quart casserole, soak rice in water for 30 minutes; drain. Add cold milk. Bake at 350° F. for 1 hour, stirring occasionally. Add sugar, salt and vanilla. Continue baking for another 30 minutes without stirring. Remove from oven and chill. Fold in chopped ginger and syrup and half of the whipped cream. Serve cold, topped with remaining whipped cream.

Serves: 8

Tel Aviv, Israel
WHIPPED CHOCOLATE BRANDY AND WINE

3 squares (3 ounces) semisweet chocolate
3 tablespoons sugar
4 eggs, separated
½ cup sweet red wine
1 teaspoon cognac
  A few drops almond extract

Melt chocolate in the top of a large double boiler. Add sugar, beaten egg yolks, wine, cognac and almond extract, beating constantly. Whip egg whites until firm and fold into chocolate mixture.

Pour into individual dessert bowls and refrigerate for at least 1 hour before serving.

Serves: 4

Tel Aviv, Israel
BRANDIED CHOCOLATE DELIGHT

6 eggs, separated
1 cup sugar, scant
5 squares (5 ounces) semisweet chocolate
¼ cup cherry brandy
3 tablespoons rum
1 tablespoon strong coffee
  Juice of 1 lemon
  Crushed walnuts

Beat egg yolks with ¼ cup of the sugar until smooth. Melt chocolate in the top of a double boiler and add to egg-yolk mixture, stirring constantly. Add cherry brandy, rum, coffee and lemon juice. Whip egg whites until stiff with remaining sugar. Fold carefully into egg-yolk and chocolate mixture.

Spoon pudding into 6 dessert dishes. Refrigerate for several hours. Sprinkle with crushed walnuts before serving.

Serves: 6

Khartoum, Sudan
DATE PUDDING

  1½ cups dates
    4 cups water
    1 teaspoon baking powder
  ¼ teaspoon salt
    5 tablespoons sugar
    5 tablespoons flour
      Melted butter

Pit dates and cut them into quarters. Boil them in 3 cups of the water. Add baking powder, salt, sugar; boil 20 minutes. Dissolve flour in 1 remaining cup of water. Mix date mixture in an electric mixer for 3 minutes, gradually adding flour solution. Mix well until thick.

Serve hot in individual dessert dishes with a little melted butter on top. *Serves: 4*

Khartoum, Sudan
APRICOT FILLETS PUDDING

  2 medium-size apricot fillets (thin sheets of pounded apricots)
  ½ cup golden raisins
  5 tablespoons sugar
  4 cups water
  3 tablespoons flour

Cut fillets into small pieces and boil them with raisins and sugar in 3 cups water for 20 minutes. Mix flour in 1 remaining cup water. Blend apricot mixture in an electric mixer, gradually adding the flour mixture. Mix well.

Pour into a bowl and chill. Serve cold.

Serves: 4

Tunis, Tunisia
BOUZA

  1 cup sorghum flour
  2⅔ cups water
  3 ounces (90 grams) shelled almonds
  3 ounces shelled hazelnuts
  2 cups milk, boiled
  1 cup castor sugar
  2 tablespoons distilled geranium water

Sift sorghum flour. Add a little water and mix to a thick dough. Pound thoroughly. Add 2⅔ cups water to dough and put mixture through a very fine sieve. Remove anything that will not go through the sieve and collect the liquid in a fairly large pan.

Blanch almonds by dipping them in boiling water for a few minutes, then remove the skins. Put them to roast. Also roast hazelnuts and remove the skins. Pound dried nuts carefully and put through a fine sieve. Place the pan over the heat, add boiled milk, castor sugar and dried nuts. Keep stirring until mixture achieves the consistency of thick cream. Add geranium water and serve. *Serves: 4*

Tunis, Tunisia
MHALBYA
(Rice Pudding)

½ pound (225 grams) rice, uncooked
1¼ cups water
3½ cups fresh milk
½ pound castor sugar
¼ cup shelled almonds
3 tablespoons shelled pistachio nuts
¼ cup shelled hazelnuts
2 tablespoons distilled geranium water

Wash rice carefully and drain. Pour 1¼ cups water and an equivalent amount of the milk into a saucepan and heat gently. Add rice and stir with a wooden spoon. Mix in sugar and keep stirring, adding the remainder of the milk gradually as the liquid is absorbed. (To tell when rice is ready, place a small mound on a dry plate, and it if does not run when the plate is turned on its side, it is cooked.) Roast and chop the nuts.

Heap rice into shallow dishes, garnish with nuts, cover with geranium water and serve.

Serves: 4

Tel Aviv, Israel
BRANDIED RICE PUDDING

3 cups milk
1 cup water
1¾ cups rice, uncooked
3 tablespoons vanilla extract
2 teaspoons almond extract
⅔ cup sugar
3 bananas, peeled
2 apples, peeled, cored and seeded
2 tangerines, peeled and seeded
1 teaspoon cherry brandy
1 cup light cream
3 tablespoons grated coconut
3 tablespoons pine nuts

Scald milk. Add water, rice, vanilla and almond extract. Cover and cook over a low heat until rice is tender but not completely cooked. Reserve 2 tablespoons of the sugar and add the rest to rice mixture. Bring to a boil. When rice is cooked through, set aside to cool in a mixing bowl.

Purée prepared fruit in a blender. Add brandy and remaining sugar, combining thoroughly. Mix fruit purée with reserved rice. Transfer to a serving dish.

Before serving, pour cream over rice pudding. Garnish with grated coconut and pine nuts.

Serves: 4

Tel Aviv, Israel
SWEET RICE

5 cups rice, uncooked
8 cups water
1 cup sugar
2 teaspoons cinnamon
½ teaspoon grated lemon rind
⅓ cup dates, chopped
1 cup walnuts, shelled and chopped

Place rice in a large saucepan and cover with 8 cups of water. Add sugar, cinnamon and lemon rind. Cook over medium heat, stirring constantly, until rice is cooked. Stir in dates and heat through.

Serve hot in individual bowls, garnished with chopped walnuts.

Serves: 6

FARINA NUT PUDDING

 1 cup sugar
 1 cup milk
 1 cup water
 2 tablespoons butter
 1 cup farina
 2 tablespoons pine nuts
 Cinnamon

Mix sugar, milk and water. Boil until it forms a syrup, remove from heat and cool. Melt butter in a heavy saucepan, add farina and pine nuts. Sauté over low heat until nuts are slightly brown. Pour cool syrup over hot farina mixture and stir well. Cover pan and cook gently until syrup has been absorbed, stirring constantly. Remove pan from heat. Wrap pan lid in a towel and replace on pan to absorb excess moisture. Leave for 30 minutes.

Before serving, stir well and sprinkle with cinnamon. *Serves: 6 to 8*

NATILLAS WITH PESTINOS

 6 cups milk
 1 cinnamon stick
 8 egg yolks
 1 cup sugar
 1 tablespoon cinnamon
 1 8-inch piece pastry dough, fried

In a double boiler, warm milk with cinnamon stick. Beat egg yolks and sugar together and add slowly to milk. Stir constantly until mixture becomes thick and creamy. Pour into a bowl, sprinkle with cinnamon and cover with fried pastry. *Serves: 6*

TURKISH FLOUR PUDDING

 1 cup sugar
 6 tablespoons rice flour
 4 teaspoons cornstarch
 4 cups milk
 5 teaspoons rose water
 4 almond macaroons

Blend sugar, rice flour and cornstarch together thoroughly in a large saucepan. Add milk, mix well, and cook over medium heat, stirring constantly, for about 10 minutes. Reduce heat and cook slowly. At this stage do not stir, as the flour paste has to settle and form a caramel. From time to time, dip spoon into the mixture; when spoon begins to stick to caramel at the bottom, increase heat slightly until spoon smells of caramel.

Remove from heat and add rose water. Place macaroons in an ovenware dish and pour hot mixture over them. Scrape caramel from pan and add to pudding. Allow to cool for about 3 hours and serve cold. *Serves: 4*

MEALIE MEAL (CORNMEAL) PUDDING

 1 cup cornmeal
 1¼ cups milk
 3 teaspoons sugar
 Pinch of salt
 1 egg, separated

Make a soft paste of cornmeal and ¼ cup of the milk. Boil together remaining milk with the sugar and salt. Stir in cornmeal paste and simmer until cooked. Remove from heat and stir in egg yolk, then fold in egg white. Can be served hot or cold. *Serves: 2*

LIBERIAN PUDDING WITH HARD SAUCE

Pudding

1 cup butter
2 cups sugar
4-6 eggs
3 cups flour
4 teaspoons baking powder
1 cup milk
2 teaspoons vanilla extract

Cream butter and sugar together until light and fluffy. Add eggs, one at a time, to creamed butter and sugar. Add dry ingredients alternately with milk and vanilla until mixture is light and smooth.

Place pudding in a strong white-cloth bag or airtight tin and boil for 1 hour in a large pot of water. Remove container from water. Slice pudding and serve with hard sauce (below).

Hard sauce

⅓ cup butter
1 cup sugar
2 teaspoons lemon juice or vanilla extract
    or
¼ cup brandy

Cream butter. Add sugar and cream until fluffy. Add desired flavoring. Pour over warm, sliced pudding.   *Serves: 6*

DEGUGE
(Millet Pudding)

½ cup water (approximate)
2½ pounds (1.3 kilograms)
    millet or corn flour
2 cups fresh milk
1 cup sugar
1 teaspoon vanilla extract
    Pinch of salt
½ teaspoon nutmeg
1½ cups curdled (but not separated) milk

In a bowl, add water to the flour, kneading mixture until it forms into small balls about 1/5-inch in diameter. Steam over water in the top of a *couscousiere.* When it is well cooked, place it in another container and work it until the small balls are separated (they will have stuck together during cooking). Then pour fresh milk over mixture. Add sugar, vanilla, salt and nutmeg. Let stand for 30 minutes.

Add curdled milk, mixing well, and serve in glass bowls.   *Serves: 6*

WATALAPPAN

10 eggs, separated
1 pound (450 grams) *jaggery* (may be
    substituted with 2½ cups honey
    boiled down until very stiff)
2 cups thick coconut milk
    Dash of freshly grated nutmeg
    Pinch of cinnamon
½ teaspoon ground cardamom
    Pinch of salt

Beat egg yolks and whites separately and then beat well together. Mix in *jaggery* (or honey substitute), coconut milk, spices and salt.

Pour into a greased mold, cover with greased paper, and steam for about 1¼ hours, or until firm to the touch. Serve in the mold.

                        Serves: 4

RUM PUDDING WITH STRAWBERRY SAUCE

1 envelope unflavored gelatin
1 cup sugar
⅛ teaspoon salt
1 cup milk
¼ cup light cream
3 eggs separated
¼ cup light rum
1 cup heavy cream

Mix together gelatin, ½ cup of the sugar and the salt in the top of a double boiler. Add milk and light cream and scald. Beat egg yolks and gradually stir into hot mixture. Place over lightly simmering water and stir until mixture coats a metal spoon. Remove from heat, add rum and chill until partially set.

Beat egg whites until light and foamy. Gradually add remaining sugar and beat until quite stiff. Whip heavy cream and fold, together with egg whites and sugar mixture, into gelatin mixture. Pour into mold or individual serving bowls and chill several hours or overnight.

To serve, top with strawberry sauce (below).

Strawberry sauce

1½ cups strawberries
1 tablespoon cornstarch (approximate)
½ teaspoon strawberry extract
Sugar to taste

Wash, stem and slice strawberries. Crush with wooden spoon or whirl slightly in blender. Place in saucepan and stir in cornstarch mixed with a little cold water. Cook, stirring frequently, over low heat until sauce begins to thicken. Remove from heat, add strawberry extract and sugar to taste. Chill. *Serves: 6 generously*

RODGROD
(Red Pudding)

4 cups raspberries
2 cups red currants
2 cups black currants
4 cups water
½ cup cornstarch
½ cup cold water
1 cup heavy cream
1 teaspoon powdered sugar

Wash berries and currants. Place in a saucepan with 4 cups water and boil until tender. Strain through a fine sieve; return strained juice to heat and bring to a boil. Stir in cornstarch which has been dissolved in ½ cup cold water. Continue cooking over low heat until mixture thickens; remove from heat and cool.

Before serving, whip heavy cream together with powdered sugar just until it holds its shape; spoon over pudding. *Serves: 10 to 12*

Monrovia, Liberia
COCONUT-ORANGE CUSTARD

    2 cups milk
    1 cup dry bread crumbs
    2 tablespoons butter
    2 eggs, separated
    ⅓ cup granulated sugar
    ⅓ teaspoon salt
    Grated rinds of 2 oranges
    1¼ cups freshly grated coconut
    ⅓ cup powdered sugar

Bring milk to a boil. Add bread crumbs and butter to milk and allow to stand for 30 minutes. Beat egg yolks. Add granulated sugar, salt and half of the grated orange rind. Add this to bread-crumb mixture. Fold in ¾ cup of the coconut. Spoon into oiled custard cups and bake at 300° F. for 40 minutes, or until firm.

To make a meringue, whip egg whites until soft peaks form. Add powdered sugar and continue whipping until stiff. Add remaining orange rind to meringue and spread on top of custard. Sprinkle with remaining coconut and bake for 20 minutes longer.

Serves: 6

Tel Aviv, Israel
WHIPPED APPLE CUSTARD

    4 egg whites
    1 cup sugar
    1 tablespoon vinegar
    1 teaspoon cornstarch
    1 tablespoon cold apple juice
    1 teaspoon vanilla extract
    ½ teaspoon cinnamon
    2 tablespoons raisins
    1 cup applesauce
    ½ cup pecans, slivered

Whip egg whites into a thick foam. Carefully stir in ½ cup of the sugar, the vinegar, cornstarch mixed with apple juice and the vanilla. Whip again. Add remaining sugar and whip into a thick, stiff foam.

Grease individual glass baking dishes and fill with egg-white mixture. Bake at 275° F. for 1 hour. Remove from oven and set aside to cool. Combine cinnamon, raisins and applesauce and spread over the desserts. Sprinkle with slivered pecans.

Serves: 4

London
CHERRY-PORT MOLD

    2½ cups canned, pitted Bing cherries
    1 cup port wine
    1½ cups Bing cherry juice
    1½ cups cold water
    2 packages cherry-flavored gelatin
    1 cup heavy cream
    1 teaspoon powdered sugar
    1½ teaspoons vanilla extract

Drain cherries, pour port wine over, cover and refrigerate overnight. Drain port wine from cherries; reserve. Combine cherry juice and ¼ cup of the water and heat. Add gelatin and stir until completely dissolved. Add reserved port wine and remaining water; chill until slightly thickened. Fold in cherries. Pour into a 1½-quart mold and chill until firm. Before serving, whip heavy cream together with powdered sugar and vanilla.

Serves: 8 to 10

Jerusalem, Israel
WHITE WINE CUSTARD

½ cup raisins
1½ cups Rhine wine (or another
    dry white wine)
1 cup water
½ cup sugar
6-7 tablespoons prepared custard
    mix, diluted in ¼ cup water
1 egg, separated
    Juice of ½ lime
    Banana slices

Soak raisins in water for ½ hour. Drain and set aside.

Bring wine, water and sugar to a boil, stirring constantly. Combine diluted custard mix with egg yolk and add to boiling wine, stirring constantly. Cook over a low heat for 5 minutes, continuing to stir. Blend lime juice into custard mixture and remove from heat. Beat egg white until stiff and fold carefully into custard mixture. Gently stir in raisins.

Garnish with banana slices.   *Serves: 4*

Tel Aviv, Israel
JELLIED WINE CUSTARD

6 egg yolks
¼ cup sugar
2 cups dry white wine
4 teaspoons gelatin
⅓ cup warm water
½ cup pecan meats (kernals)
½ cup cherries, pitted

Beat egg yolks and sugar together until light. Add wine and blend thoroughly. Transfer to a saucepan and cook over low heat, stirring constantly, until mixture thickens. (Do not boil.) Remove thickened mixture from heat. Add gelatin, dissolved in ⅓ cup warm water, stirring constantly. Continue to stir until mixture cools.

Transfer to a dessert mold, add pecans and cherries and chill until firm. Turn out and serve.   *Serves: 4*

Mamma Leone's, New York City
ZABAGLIONE

6 egg yolks
2 tablespoons sugar
    Sweet sherry
    Sweet vermouth
    Whipped cream (optional)
4 cherries, pitted (optional)

Beat egg yolks until thoroughly mixed. Measure them. Add sugar and ¾ the measure of the egg yolks of sherry and ¼ the measure of vermouth. Cook in the top of a double boiler over hot (not boiling) water, beating constantly until mixture thickens.

Pour into dessert glasses and chill. Before serving, top with a tablespoon of whipped cream and a cherry, if desired.   *Serves: 4*

Chicago, Illinois
ZABAGLIONE MARSALA

8 egg yolks
2 egg whites
½ cup sugar
1 cup Marsala wine

In the top of a double boiler beat egg yolks and whites with sugar. When mixture is very thick and creamy, add Marsala, place the pan over simmering hot water and heat mixture gradually, never ceasing to beat with a rotary or electric beater. When the zabaglione is very thick and hot, but just before it reaches the boiling point, spoon it into glasses and serve at once.

Serves: 6

Jerusalem, Israel
APPLE AND COCONUT CUSTARD

3 cups milk
½ cup plus 2 tablespoons sugar
2 tablespoons prepared custard
    mix, diluted in a little cold water
2 egg yolks
½ cup light cream
2 large apples, peeled, cored and cut
    in large chunks
1 teaspoon lemon juice
1 tablespoon margarine
    Ladyfingers
2 tablespoons finely grated coconut
1 cup heavy cream, whipped

Boil milk with ½ cup of the sugar. Add diluted custard mix, stirring until the boiling milk thickens. Remove from heat and add egg yolks and light cream, stirring constantly. Set aside.

Steam apple chunks with remaining sugar, the lemon juice and the margarine.

Line bottom of a glass dish with ladyfingers. Pour in half of the hot custard. Top with a layer of apples. Sprinkle on coconut. Add another layer of ladyfingers and finish with remaining custard. Refrigerate.

Immediately before serving, garnish with whipped cream.

Serves: 4

Monrovia, Liberia
SWEET-POTATO CUSTARD

½ cup sugar
¾ cup butter
2 eggs, slightly beaten
1¼ cups milk
3 cups mashed and strained
    sweet potatoes
1 teaspoon vanilla extract
½ teaspoon grated nutmeg
    Whipped cream or fruit garnish
    (optional)

Cream sugar and butter together until mixture is fluffy. Add to mixture slightly beaten eggs. Add milk, sweet potatoes, vanilla and nutmeg. Stir vigorously until smooth.

Pour into greased ovenproof dish and bake at 375° F. until brown and firm. Serve warm or cold. Top with whipped cream, canned fruit or a fruit sauce, if desired.

Serves: 4 to 6

Tel Aviv, Israel
TANGERINE FLAN

3 cups tangerine juice
2 tablespoons lemon juice
1 cup water
6 tablespoons sugar
3 tablespoons prepared custard mix,
    diluted in ½ cup water
1 teaspoon finely grated tangerine rind
1 egg, separated
  Tangerine sections

Bring juices, water and sugar to a boil. Stir in diluted custard mix and cook over a low heat, stirring constantly, for 2 minutes. Remove from heat. Incorporate tangerine rind. Whip egg white; add egg yolk to it. Fold egg mixture into custard mixture.

Serve cold in individual dishes, garnished with tangerine sections.
Serves: 2

New York City
MANDARIN ORANGE AND CHOCOLATE FLUFF

¾ cup mandarin orange sections in syrup
¼ teaspoon salt
1 egg, separated
½ cup semisweet chocolate morsels
½ cup sour cream
1 tablespoon sugar
1½ tablespoons Cointreau (optional)

Drain oranges, reserving ¼ cup syrup; set aside orange sections. Combine syrup with salt and bring to a boil. Remove from heat. Beat egg yolk slightly and add to syrup mixture, stirring rapidly. Cook over medium heat for 1 minute, stirring constantly. Remove from heat. Stir in chocolate morsels until melted. Blend in sour cream. Beat egg white until stiff but not dry. Beat in sugar until egg white is stiff and glossy. Fold in chocolate mixture.

Spoon into 4 sherbet glasses. Top with reserved orange sections and Cointreau, if desired. Chill.
Serves: 4

Stockholm, Sweden
LINGONBERRY CREAM

2 eggs, slightly beaten
¼ cup flour
½ cup sugar
1½ cups small-curd cottage cheese
1 cup heavy cream
1 cup milk
1½ teaspoons almond extract
1½ cups lingonberries

Combine eggs, flour, sugar, cottage cheese, ½ cup of the cream, milk and almond extract. Pour into a 1-quart casserole dish.

Bake at 375° F. for about 50 minutes, or until set. Whip remaining cream and mound on dessert, which may be served warm or cold. Top with lingonberries.
Serves: 4

LEMON CREAM WITH RASPBERRY PUREE

1 envelope unflavored gelatin
¼ cup cold water
¾ cup granulated sugar
   Pinch of salt
1 cup boiling water
   Grated rind of 1 lemon
¼ cup lemon juice, or half lemon and
      half lime juice
3 egg whites (retain yolks for raspberry
      purée, below)
   Sliced almonds, toasted
   Shredded coconut, toasted

Soften gelatin in the cold water. Add ½ cup of the sugar, the salt and the boiling water; stir until gelatin and sugar are dissolved. Add lemon rind and juice and chill until mixture is partially firm.

Beat egg whites until stiff but not dry. Gradually add remaining sugar, beating until stiff. Add partially firmed gelatin mixture and blend thoroughly. Chill until completely firm.

Meanwhile, prepare raspberry purée (below) and toast the almonds and coconut.

To serve, spoon lemon cream into individual glasses and top with raspberry purée, toasted almonds and coconuts.

Raspberry Purée

2 cups fresh raspberries
3 egg yolks
3 tablespoons sugar
¼ cup water
¼ teaspoon vanilla extract

Purée raspberries in a blender. In the top of a double boiler, combine egg yolks, sugar, water and purée. Cook over hot, not boiling, water until mixture thickens, stirring constantly. Remove from heat and stir in vanilla. Chill thoroughly. *Serves: 6 generously*

FROZEN RUM-RAISIN CREAM

1 cup milk
2 eggs, beaten
⅓ cup sugar
   Pinch of salt
½ cup heavy cream, whipped
½ cup raisins, chopped
¼ cup light rum
1 banana, mashed

In the top of a double boiler, heat milk quickly over boiling water. In a bowl, combine eggs, sugar and salt. Gradually stir in hot milk. Return mixture to top of double boiler and cook, stirring constantly, over simmering water, until mixture coats a metal spoon. Remove from heat and allow to cool. Fold in whipped cream and freeze until partially firm.

Meanwhile, soak raisins in the rum. Combine raisins and rum with mashed banana and fold into partially frozen custard. Freeze until firm.
Serves: 4

POTS DE CREME

BOURBON ON A CLOUD

3 cups heavy cream
½ cup sugar
1 tablespoon vanilla extract
5 egg yolks
1 square (1 ounce) semisweet chocolate
    Whipped cream
2 teaspoons confectioners' sugar

1 egg, separated
¼ cup bourbon
⅓ envelope unflavored gelatin
¼ cup sugar
⅛ cup chopped walnuts
⅓ cup heavy cream, whipped
    Fresh strawberries

Preheat oven to 325° F. In a medium-sized saucepan, combine cream and ½ cup sugar. Cook over medium heat, stirring frequently, until sugar is dissolved and mixture is hot. Remove from heat and stir in vanilla. Beat egg yolks until blended but not frothy; gradually add hot mixture, stirring constantly. Strain.

Pour into ten 3-ounce (90-gram) pot-de-crème cups. Set cups in a baking pan with ½ inch hot water in the bottom. Bake for 25 minutes, or until mixture begins to set around edges. Immediately remove cups from water and place on a wire rack. Allow to cool for ½ hour; refrigerate covered for at least 4 hours.

For chocolate curls, draw vegetable scraper across flat surface of chocolate square. (Lift curls with wooden toothpick to avoid breaking.) Top each cream cup with chocolate curls and sweetened whipped cream.   *Serves: 10*

In the top of a double boiler, beat egg yolk slightly. Gradually add bourbon, stirring constantly. (Addition of bourbon too quickly tends to "cook" the egg yolk.) Set aside. Combine gelatin and half of the sugar; mix well. Add egg yolk mixture to gelatin. Cook over hot (not boiling) water, stirring constantly, until mixture coats a metal spoon — about 10 minutes. Beat egg white until foamy. Gradually add remaining sugar and continue beating until stiff and glossy. Fold in yolk mixture. Chill for 20 minutes.

Fold in walnuts and whipped cream. Turn into a 3-cup mold. Chill until firm. Unmold. Serve garnished with strawberries.   *Serves: 2 to 4*

Barcelona, Spain
CARAMEL CREAM

¾ cup sugar
4 eggs
2 cups milk
1 stick cinnamon
1 teaspoon vanilla extract
Pinch of salt

Caramelize ¼ cup of the sugar by cooking in a saucepan, stirring constantly, until golden brown. While still hot, pour evenly into bottom of 4 individual overproof dishes. Allow to cool.

Beat eggs until frothy. Gradually add remaining sugar, beating constantly. Scald milk with cinnamon stick. Gradually add hot milk to egg mixture, stirring until sugar is completely dissolved. Add vanilla and salt. Pour into prepared dishes. Place dishes in a pan of hot water and bake at 375° F. for 1 hour. Chill.   *Serves: 4*

Moira Hotel, Dublin, Ireland
CREME CARAMEL "SIOBHAN"

½ cup sugar
2 tablespoons water
3 eggs
2 tablespoons sugar
2 cups milk
1 teaspoon vanilla extract
½ cup crème de menthe
1 cup heavy cream

Make caramel by boiling ½ cup sugar and water until it takes on a mahogany color. Pour into 4 individual ramekins or one large tin mold. Allow to set. Beat eggs, sugar and milk together. Add vanilla. Strain custard into the molds.

Place molds in a dish of water so that the water comes a quarter of the way up. Bake at 250° F. in oven until set. Cool. Unmold and serve with crème de menthe and heavy cream on top.
     Serves: 4

Lyons, France
MARRONS AUX MOUSQUETAIRES

1½ cups vanilla pudding
1¾ cups light cream
½ cup Armagnac
    Juice of 1 lemon
1 lemon rind, grated
1 1-pound (450 gram) can sweetened
    chestnut purée
6 tablespoons soft butter
2 egg yolks
2 egg whites, stiffly beaten
½ cup finely chopped pecans
1 9-ounce (250 gram) jar whole
    chestnuts packed in heavy syrup

Combine vanilla pudding, cream, Armagnac, lemon juice and rind and beat until smooth. Chill until slightly thickened.

While custard sauce is chilling, mash chestnut purée. Stir in butter and egg yolks. Fold in egg whites and pecans. Spoon mixture into a well-buttered 3-cup casserole.

Bake at 350° F. for 40 minutes, or until browned and puffed. Serve dessert warm with chilled custard sauce. Garnish with whole chestnuts in syrup.
     Serves: 8

Grand Sofia, Sophia, Bulgaria
BULGARIAN CREAM

1½ tablespoons unflavored gelatin
3 tablespoons cold water
1¼ cups milk
4 egg yolks
1 cup sugar
2 teaspoons vanilla extract
1 tablespoon liqueur
1 tablespoon rum
½ cup jam
¼ cup macaroon crumbs
1 cup heavy cream
1 cup whipped cream
⅔ cup Velvet Chocolate Sauce
(see p. 184)

Soften gelatin in the cold water. Beat together milk, egg yolks, sugar and softened gelatin. Heat to the boiling point, but do not allow to boil. Strain and cool until slightly set. Stir in vanilla, liqueur, rum, jam, macaroon crumbs and cream.

Pour into individual molds and cool. Serve decorated with whipped cream and Velvet Chocolate Sauce.

Serves: 5

Zürich, Switzerland
"LACED" CHOCOLATE BAVARIAN

¼ cup semisweet chocolate morsels
4 tablespoons light brown sugar,
firmly packed
1 tablespoon water
¼ envelope (¾ tablespoon)
unflavored gelatin
1 egg, separated
1½ tablespoons bourbon
Pinch of salt
¼ cup heavy cream, whipped
½ cup coarsely crumbled crisp
cinnamon-flavored wafers
Additional whipped cream (optional)

In the top of a double boiler, combine chocolate, half the brown sugar, the water and the gelatin. Cook over hot (not boiling) water, stirring constantly, until gelatin is dissolved and chocolate is melted. Add egg yolk and bourbon and beat until blended. Remove from oven water. Beat egg white and salt until foamy. Gradually add remaining brown sugar and beat until stiff and glossy. Fold egg-white mixture, whipped cream and wafer crumbs into chocolate mixture.

Pour into sherbet glasses and chill until firm. If desired, serve garnished with additional whipped cream.

Serves: 2 to 3

Zürich, Switzerland
BAVARIAN CREAM

- ½ envelope unflavored gelatin
- ½ cup milk
- 2 eggs, separated
- ½ cup sugar
-   Pinch of salt
- 1 teaspoon vanilla extract
- ½ cup heavy cream, whipped

Soften gelatin in milk in the top of a double boiler. Beat egg yolks and add with half of the sugar and the salt to gelatin. Cook over simmering (not boiling) water, stirring constantly until thickened and smooth. Add vanilla and cool. Stir frequently to prevent a skin from forming over the top. Beat egg whites until peaks form, add the remaining sugar gradually and continue beating until mixture is glossy. Fold into custard. Fold in whipped cream. Pour into mold or individual glasses; chill until firm.

May be served plain or with fresh berries or a liqueur. *Serves: 4*

Hotel Pension Schwarzenberg, Vienna, Austria
SCHMANKERLBOMBE

Schmankerl

- ½ cup milk
- 1 cup flour
- ½ cup sugar
- 1 tablespoon butter, for baking

Make a thick paste from milk and flour; add sugar. Butter baking sheet and spread the paste thinly on to it with a spatula. (It should be thin enough to read through.) Bake at 250° F. until brown. Remove from baking sheet and, when cold, break into small pieces.

Strawberry sauce

- 2 cups strawberries, fresh or frozen
- ½ cup water
- ½ cup sugar
- 1 tablespoon butter, for baking

Boil strawberries in water with sugar. Sieve and chill.

Conclusion

- 1 cup heavy cream, whipped
- 1 cup Bavarian Cream

Blend whipped cream, Bavarian Cream and pieces of schmankerl together. Pour into a large charlotte mold. Allow filled mold to remain in the freezer for at least 3 hours. Serve with strawberry sauce. *Serves: 4*

Top of the Town, Hotel Inter-Continental,
Auckland, New Zealand
CHOCOLATE MOUSSE

½ pound (225 grams) chocolate
2 tablespoons milk
2 tablespoons cognac
3 tablespoons sugar
2 tablespoons freshly ground almonds
4 eggs, separated

Melt chocolate with milk and cognac; add sugar and ground almonds. Cool slightly and briskly stir in egg yolks. Let stand for a few minutes, then gently fold in stiffly beaten egg whites.

Pour into individual dishes and chill well before serving.
Serves: 4 to 6

Maison Lafite, New Orleans, Louisiana
MOUSSE AU CHOCOLATE

½ cup sugar
4 tablespoons dark rum
½ pound (225 grams) semisweet chocolate
2 egg whites
2 cups heavy cream
Grated chocolate for garnish

In a small saucepan, cook sugar and rum over a very low heat until sugar melts and becomes a syrup. Do not let it turn brown. Break chocolate into small pieces, melt in the top of a double boiler. When chocolate is smooth, add syrup (syrup and chocolate should be about the same temperature). Stir vigorously with a wooden spoon. If mixture is too heavy, add lukewarm water until smooth. Beat egg whites until they are stiff. Whip the heavy cream. Combine. Fold chocolate into mixture.

Chill and grate some chocolate on top before serving.
Serves: 4

Steer Palace, New York City
STEER PALACE BANANA MOUSSE

½ cup sugar
1 tablespoon cornstarch
Dash of salt
3 large egg yolks
1½ cups light cream
½ teaspoon vanilla extract
4 ripe bananas, peeled
Juice of 1 lemon
1 cup heavy cream, whipped

Combine sugar, cornstarch and salt in the top of a double boiler. Beat in egg yolks and ¼ cup of the light cream. Add remaining cream and heat only until hot — do not boil. Add vanilla extract. Stir and cook until custard is thick, over simmering (not boiling) water. Cool, stirring frequently to prevent a skin from forming over the top. Mash bananas with lemon juice and blend in mixture. Fold in 1½ cups of the whipped cream.

Fill in champagne glasses. Garnish top with remaining whipped cream and chill for ½ hour before serving.
Serves: 6

PEAR-ALMOND MOUSSE

2 cups heavy cream
½ cup sugar
1 tablespoon unflavored gelatin, softened in ½ cup cold water
½ cup boiling water
2 egg yolks, beaten
2 tablespoons pear brandy
2 medium-size fresh pears
¼ cup sliced almonds
1 cup chocolate sauce (see p. 184)

Whip cream with ⅓ cup of the sugar. Dissolve softened gelatin in boiling water. Beat egg yolks with the remaining sugar and the brandy for about 5 minutes. Peel, core and slice pears. Toast sliced almonds. Stir dissolved gelatin into egg mixture, add pears and almonds and fold into whipped cream.

Pour into a 1½-quart mold and chill for 2 hours.

Just before serving, pour 1 cup warm chocolate sauce over mousse. (For a quick chocolate topping, melt 1 cup of extra-rich chocolate ice cream and pour over mousse just before serving.) *Serves: 6*

HAZELNUT MOUSSE

2 cups milk
1½ cups sugar
6 egg yolks
1 tablespoon granulated gelatin
1 cup roasted hazelnuts
3 cups heavy cream, whipped
Mousse au Chocolate (see p. 134)

Boil milk and ½ cup of the sugar in a saucepan. Once boiling, add milk mixture to egg yolks in a bowl, stirring constantly. Return mixture back into saucepan and stir until it thickens over low heat, but do not boil or it will separate. Remove from heat. Soften gelatin in 1 teaspoon of cold water and add to mixture. Let cool. Boil remaining sugar and 2 tablespoons water. When sugar is golden, add roasted hazelnuts and mix well. Remove from heat and pour on oiled tray. Let cool until hard, then grind it coarsely.

Mix hazelnut mixture with 2 cups of the whipped cream and Mousse au Chocolate. Fill into champagne glasses. Garnish top with remaining whipped cream and chill. *Serves: 8*

Tel Aviv, Israel
APPLE MERINGUE WITH CUSTARD SAUCE

8 firm apples
4 egg whites
⅔ cup sugar
½ teaspoon Curaçao brandy
¼ teaspoon salt

Wash and core apples. Cook in boiling water until tender; drain. Transfer to a baking dish.

Whip egg whites until firm with sugar, Curaçao brandy and salt. Spoon over apples and bake at 350° F. for 15 minutes. Meanwhile, prepare the sauce (below).

Custard sauce

1½ cups milk
½ teaspoon vanilla extract
½ teaspoon almond extract
4 egg yolks
3 tablespoons sugar

Boil the milk, then add vanilla and almond extract. In a bowl, beat together egg yolks and sugar. Transfer to a saucepan, over low heat, and add the milk, stirring constantly. When mixture has thickened, remove from heat, set aside to cool and refrigerate.

Pass sauce separately. *Serves: 8*

The George Hotel, Haddington, Scotland
FRUIT COCKTAIL MERINGUE

4 cups mixed sliced fresh fruit
½ pound (225 grams) sponge cake
4 egg whites
¼ teaspoon lemon juice
¼ teaspoon salt
6 tablespoons sugar

Place fruit in a shallow ovenproof dish. Arrange slices of cake evenly on top of fruit.

Place egg whites, lemon juice and salt in a large mixing bowl. Whisk until stiff. Fold in 4 tablespoons of the sugar and continue beating for 5 minutes. Fold in remaining sugar and beat until sugar is completely dissolved.

Pipe or spread meringue over prepared fruit and cake. Bake at 250° F. for 1 hour, until meringue is dry, or bake at 400° F. until meringue is browned. *Serves: 8*

Tour Eiffel, Paris
SURPRISE TOUR EIFFEL
(Meringue with Mirabelle Brandy)

  1 cup sugar
  2 egg yolks
  1 teaspoon vanilla extract, or
     1 pulverized vanilla bean
  4 ladyfingers, or 4 slices sponge cake
  ¼ cup kirsch
  8 scoops vanilla ice cream
12 egg whites
  ½ cup Mirabelle brandy

Make a paste with ½ cup of the sugar, the egg yolks and vanilla extract or a bit of pulverized vanilla bean. Set aside.

Soak ladyfingers or cake slices in kirsch. Top them with scoops of vanilla ice cream.

Beat egg whites to a stiff froth with remaining sugar; gently mix in egg-sugar paste. Keep beating until very stiff. Spread meringue on ice cream with a steel spatula, shaping each dessert like a baked Alaska. Reserve enough meringue to decorate, using a fluted tip on a pastry bag.

Bake at 450° F. for about 5 minutes, or just until the meringue is browned. Before serving, pour Mirabelle brandy over baked desserts and ignite them. (A good tip to make rum or brandy flame: warm it first.)   *Serves: 4*

Royal Hotel, Copenhagen, Denmark
CORBEILLE "ROYAL"
(Meringue Baskets)

2 egg whites
½ cup sugar
½ cup semisweet chocolate
2 tablespoons coffee liqueur
1 teaspoon instant coffee
¼ cup heavy cream, whipped
½ cup broken, roasted nuts

Beat egg whites until foamy. Add sugar gradually, beating well after each addition until all sugar is dissolved. Continue beating until meringue is very stiff and shiny. Form into a basket shape on damp brown paper on a cookie sheet. Dry in oven at 250° F. until firm but not browned.

Melt chocolate and pour out on a buttered cookie sheet or plate. While still soft, cut a circle the size of the meringue basket with a cookie cutter. Also cut a strip long enough to become the "handle" of the basket. Let cool but do not chill.

Add liqueur and instant coffee to whipped cream and blend in gently.

To assemble, place chocolate round on serving plate. Place meringue basket on top of chocolate. Sprinkle meringue with nuts, reserving some, and fill the basket with the flavored whipped cream. Attach chocolate "handle" and sprinkle all with reserved nuts.

Serves: 1

PEACH ALCRON MERINGUE

3 cups fresh peach slices
2 tablespoons lemon juice
2 cups milk
5 eggs, separated
1½ cups powdered sugar
10 ladyfingers, split lengthwise
2 tablespoons Curaçao
¼ cup grated bitter chocolate
¼ cup heavy cream, whipped
½ cup sugar
¼ cup slivered toasted almonds

Sprinkle peach slices with lemon juice to preserve fresh color.

Prepare custard by mixing milk, egg yolk and powdered sugar in the top of a double boiler. Cook over simmering water, stirring constantly until custard thickens. Cool.

In a buttered heatproof serving dish, arrange ladyfingers, split-side down, in one layer. Sprinkle with Curaçao and grated chocolate. Place drained peach slices on ladyfinger layer. Mix custard and whipped cream and pour over.

Beat egg whites until foamy. Add ½ cup sugar, a little at a time, and continue beating until glossy. Spread over custard. Sprinkle with almonds. Bake at 400° F. for about 10 minutes, or until meringue is lightly browned. Serve hot or chilled. *Serves: 10*

Gaston et Gastounette, Cannes, France
LE SECRET DES MOINES
(Monk's Secret)

4 egg whites (½ cup)
¼ cup powdered sugar, sifted
1 teaspoon vanilla extract
¾ cup cake flour
12 ladyfingers
½ cup Lerina or other liqueur
6 tablespoons chopped candied fruit
6 scoops vanilla ice cream
½ cup heavy cream, whipped and slightly
    sweetened
   Bitter chocolate, slivered into curls
   Candied cherries

Butter and flour a cookie sheet and set aside. Prepare a pastry bag with a fairly large plain tip.

Beat egg whites until foamy. Add sugar, beating after each spoonful until it is completely absorbed. Continue beating until egg whites stand in stiff, shiny peaks. Blend in vanilla.

Sift flour twice. Add to meringue mixture in 3 parts, quickly and gently folding after each addition. Fill pastry bag and shape 6 cup-shaped pastries on the prepared cookie sheet. Dry in the oven at 200° F. for about 40 minutes. Cool completely.

Break 2 ladyfingers into each pastry cup. Moisten with liqueur. Add candied fruit, then a scoop of ice cream. Top with sweetened whipped cream, chocolate curls and a cherry. *Serves: 6*

Maile Restaurant, Kahala Hilton, Honolulu, Hawaii
MAILE TARTS

2¼ cups sugar
¼ cup sliced roasted almonds
1 cup candied fruits
1½ cups canned pineapple, chopped
3 tablespoons Grand Marnier
2 tablespoons kirshwasser
¾ cup water
6 egg whites
2 cups heavy cream
Pinch of salt
4 pineapple slices
Maraschino cherries for garnish

Melt half the sugar in a shallow pan until brown. Add almonds and mix. Pour mixture on a cold stainless steel tray to cool. When hard, crush with a rolling pin until almost powdery.

Marinate candied fruits and chopped pineapple in Grand Marnier and kirshwasser. Slowly boil remaining half of the sugar and ¾ cup water until syrupy. To prevent crystallization of sugar, do not stir while boiling. Whip egg whites until stiff peaks form. Slowly pour syrup over meringue and continue whipping until cold. Whip heavy cream. Set aside some whipped cream for garnish.

Fold whipped cream, candied fruits, pineapple, crushed caramel and salt into meringue mixture. Pour into 2 pie plates and freeze. Garnish meringue tarts with slice of pineapple, remaining whipped cream and maraschino cherries. The second meringue tart can be kept frozen 2 to 3 weeks. *Yield: 2 meringue tarts*

London Tavern, London Hilton Hotel, London
SNOWBALLS

6 eggs, separated
1¼ cups sugar
2½ cups milk
1 teaspoon vanilla extract

Beat egg whites with 1 cup of the sugar to make a stiff, glossy meringue. Form into 6 or 8 round meringues and poach in barely simmering water until firm. Turn meringues to poach evenly. Remove with a slotted spoon and drain well. Place in a large serving bowl and chill.

Scald milk — it must not boil — then beat in egg yolks, remaining ¼ cup of sugar and vanilla. Bring to just below boiling point. Allow to get cold, and then pour over chilled snowballs. Serve very cold. *Serves: 6 to 8*

COFFEE-CUP SOUFFLE

SOUFFLE PRALINE AUX AMANDES

4½ tablespoons flour
4½ tablespoons butter
1½ cups milk
6 eggs, separated
3 teaspoons instant coffee
1 cup sugar
4 tablespoons coffee ice cream

Mix flour with butter until mixture is smooth. Place milk in a saucepan and bring almost to a boil. Add butter-flour mixture and stir until thick. Allow to cool.

Add egg yolks and instant coffee to cooled mixture. Beat egg whites until they form soft peaks. Continue beating, gradually adding ¾ cup of the sugar, until stiff peaks form. Fold gently into mixture.

Butter the insides of 6 ovenproof coffee cups and sprinkle lightly with remaining sugar. Setting aside 4 tablespoons of the soufflé mixture, divide remaining soufflé between prepared coffee cups. Bake at 425° F. for about 11 minutes. (Eleven minutes will produce a soufflé of medium consistency. Shorten or lengthen baking time a few minutes if a softer or firmer consistency is desired.)

Serve with a sauce made by mixing the reserved soufflé mixture with coffee ice cream.

Serves: 6

4 tablespoons flour
4 tablespoons butter
1 cup boiled milk
6 eggs, separated
6 tablespoons almond paste
¾ cup sugar
Chopped almonds
Vanilla sauce (optional)

Work flour into the butter until a smooth paste is formed. Pour milk into paste. Add egg yolks and continue stirring until a smooth batter is formed. Add almond paste. Beat egg whites to a firm stage with sugar and incorporate into mixture.

Pour batter into individual soufflé molds, which have been buttered and sprinkled with sugar and flour. Add almonds on top and bake at 350° F. for 30 minutes. Serve with vanilla sauce, if desired.

Serves: 2

SOUFFLE LAPEROUSE

12 eggs, separated
1½ cups sugar
⅔ cup sifted flour
4 cups milk
1 vanilla bean
1 cup caramelized sugar
2 tablespoons rum
⅔ cup candied fruit
Sugar
Additional rum (optional)

Mix egg yolks with sugar and sifted flour. Bring milk to a boil with vanilla bean. When milk starts to boil, stir egg-yolk mixture into it. Beat very well to make a smooth batter. Bring batter to a rolling boil again and set it aside immediately. To this batter add caramelized sugar, rum and candied fruit. Beat egg whites until they form stiff, shiny peaks and fold them into batter.

Butter and sprinkle a large soufflé dish with sugar. Pour soufflé into dish and bake at 350° F. for about 20 minutes. Soufflé should be fairly firm when done.

When ready to serve, sprinkle some sugar over soufflé and let the top caramelize quickly under the broiler. The top of the soufflé may also be pricked a little and moistened with additional rum, if desired.   *Serves: 12*

BEIGNET SOUFFLES

½ cup water
¼ cup butter
½ cup flour
1 tablespoon sugar
Pinch of salt
3 eggs
Oil for deep frying
½ cup sugar
1 teaspoon cinnamon

Boil water and butter. When butter has melted, add flour, sugar and salt all at once. Remove from direct heat and stir vigorously until paste leaves sides of pan.

Pipe paste through pastry bag with a plain tube into rounds, or drop by heaping teaspoonfuls, into 370° F. deep frying oil. Soufflés will gradually swell to 4 or 5 times their original size and when cooked will be golden brown and hollow inside.

Remove soufflés from fat and roll them in sugar mixed with cinnamon. Set aside to cool.

Conclusion

½ cup heavy cream, whipped
2 tablespoons grated orange peel
1 tablespoon honey
1 cup custard sauce
2 tablespoons brandy

When soufflés are completely cold, fill with whipped cream mixed with grated orange peel and honey. Serve with lukewarm custard sauce mixed with brandy.   *Serves: 4*

SOUFFLE A LA NAPOLEON

Hotel Napoléon, Paris

Crème pâtissière

> 2 cups milk
> ½ teaspoon vanilla extract
> 6 egg yolks (reserve whites)
> 1 cup sugar
> ¼ cup flour

Boil milk with vanilla; while milk is boiling, mix with a whip the egg yolks, sugar and flour. While milk is still boiling, add mixture and whip over the heat, mixing it constantly to avoid sticking for 5 minutes.

This recipe makes enough crème for at least 6 individual soufflés. It can also be used for filling eclairs, etc.

Soufflé

For each person to be served, you will need:

> 6 tablespoons crème pâtissière
> 2 tablespoons candied fruit
> 1 tablespoon kirsch
> 2 egg whites
> 1 teaspoon sugar
> 1 soufflé dish, buttered and sugared

In a bowl, mix crème pâtissière, fruit and kirsch. Whip egg whites with sugar until thick like whipped cream. Mix slowly with a spoon into the crème mixture. Return back into egg whites and mix gently.

Pour into individual soufflé dish and bake at 450° F. for 15 minutes.

SOUFFLE AUX FRAISES

Avignon, France

> ½ cup milk
> ½ cup light cream
> 4 tablespoons granulated sugar
> 4 tablespoons sifted flour
> 4 egg yolks
> 3 ounces (90 grams) strawberry preserves
> 1 pound (450 grams) fresh strawberries
> 4 tablespoons powdered sugar
> 6 egg whites
> Vanilla sauce (optional)
> Kirschwasser (optional)

Bring to a slow rolling boil the milk, cream and granulated sugar. Add sifted flour and continue to cook. Stir for 3 minutes. Remove from stove and add egg yolks, strawberry preserves and fresh strawberries presoaked in the powdered sugar. Stiffly beat egg whites and fold lightly into mixture.

Butter and sugar the inside surface of a soufflé ramekin and pour in soufflé mixture. Bake at 350° F. for 20 to 25 minutes. Serve with prepared vanilla sauce, flavored with kirschwasser, if desired.

Serves: 4

Madrid Restaurant, Rizal, Philippines
ORANGE SOUFFLE

> ¼ cup butter
> 6 tablespoons flour
>   Dash of salt
> 1 cup milk
> ¼ cup orange-juice concentrate
> ½ cup water
> 1½ teaspoons grated lemon peel
> 6 eggs, separated
> ¼ cup sugar

Melt butter; blend in flour and salt. Gradually stir in milk and cook over low heat, stirring constantly until thick. Remove from heat.

Measure ¼ cup orange-juice concentrate from a 6-ounce can (reserve remainder for orange sauce); combine with water and grated lemon peel. Stir into hot mixture. Beat egg yolks until thick and lemon colored. Gradually add hot mixture; mix well and let cool somewhat. Meanwhile beat egg whites to soft peaks; gradually add sugar and beat until stiff peaks form. Fold yolk mixture into egg whites.

Pour into ungreased 1½-quart casserole with a paper collar. Set dish in shallow pan filled to a depth of 1 inch with hot water. Bake at 325° F. for about 1½ hours, or until knife inserted comes out clean. Peel off paper. Serve at once, breaking apart gently with two forks. Pass orange sauce (below) separately.

Orange sauce

> ½ cup sugar
> 1½ tablespoons cornstarch
>   Dash of salt
> ½ cup orange-juice concentrate
> 1 cup water
> 1 tablespoon butter

Combine sugar, cornstarch and salt. Stir in orange-juice concentrate and water. Cook and stir until thick. Stir in butter. Serve warm.

Serves: 8

New York City
SOUFFLE ORANGERIE

> 8 large oranges
> 8 teaspoons currant jelly
> 8 egg yolks
> 1 cup sugar
>   Grated rind of 2 oranges
> 4 tablespoons Grand Marnier
> 2 cups heavy cream, whipped
> 1 tablespoon sifted confectioners' sugar

Cut a slice across each orange about a quarter from the top; scoop out fruit. Spoon 1 teaspoon currant jelly into bottom of each orange shell. In top of a double boiler, beat egg yolks and sugar together over hot, not boiling, water until thick and foamy. Remove from heat but continue beating until cool. Blend in orange rind, Grand Marnier and about ¾ of the whipped cream. Spoon equal amounts of mixture into each orange shell; freeze. Sweeten remaining whipped cream slightly with confectioners' sugar.

Just before serving, pipe or spoon rosette of sweetened whipped cream over each orange.

Serves: 4

SOUFFLE FORT ROYALE

4 tablespoons butter
2 tablespoons flour
1 cup light cream
5 egg yolks
6 egg whites

4 tablespoons sugar
5 tablespoons Grand Marnier
Additional Grand Marnier
8 ladyfingers
Glazed oranges, chopped

In a saucepan melt butter; add flour and cook for a short time until mixture colors. Add cream after it has been heated to a boiling point. Stir mixture constantly, cooking for 5 minutes. Beat 5 egg yolks and sugar. Stir this into mixture. Add Grand Marnier. Fold in 6 egg whites which have been beaten stiffly.

In a well-buttered and sugared soufflé dish, pour in half of the mixture. Soak ladyfingers in additional Grand Marnier and spread them out on top of the mixture. Spread chopped glazed oranges, soaked in additional Grand Marnier, over ladyfingers. Cover with remaining half of soufflé mixture. Bake at 450° F. for 10 to 12 minutes. Lower heat to 350° F. and bake for 20 minutes more. *Serves: 4*

SOUFFLE GLACE FRAMBOISINE
(Frozen Raspberry Soufflé)

½ cup raspberry juice
½ cup sugar
4 egg yolks
1⅔ cups heavy cream

6 tablespoons milk
1 tablespoon raspberry liqueur
½ cup heavy cream, whipped
½ cup fresh raspberries

Boil raspberry juice with sugar to make a syrup. Add egg yolks; beat well with wire whisk. Let cool.

Beat cream and milk until softly whipped. Add raspberry liqueur and syrup-egg mixture and blend gently. Pour mixture into a soufflé dish and place in the freezer for 6 hours.

Before serving, decorate soufflé with whipped cream and fresh raspberries. *Serves: 6*

Claude Monet, *Women in a Garden*, 1866-7

Camille Pissarro, *Red Roofs*, 1877

Grenoble, France
SOUFFLE FRAMBOIS

4 tablespoons Crème Pâtissière (see p. 172)
3 egg yolks
5 egg whites
½ cup raspberries
¼ cup kirsch
4 pieces Génoise sponge cake (see p. 6)

Combine Crème Pâtissière with egg yolks. Whisk egg whites into a firm froth and fold into above mixture. Marinate raspberries in kirsch. Place raspberries on pieces of génoise in each of 4 individual soufflé molds and cover with soufflé mixture. Bake at 300° F. for 15 minutes.

Serves: 4

Altanta, Georgia

STRAWBERRY-LIME PUNCH

5 10-ounce (280-gram) packages frozen strawberries, sliced and partially thawed
½ cup currant jelly
½ cup lime juice
4 cups finely crushed ice
4 cups water
1 large lime, thinly sliced

Combine half the strawberries with half the currant jelly and half the lime juice in a blender; beat until smooth. Pour into a large punch bowl. Repeat same process with remaining strawberries, jelly and juice. Stir in crushed ice and water and float lime slices on top.

Serves: 12 to 15

Maurice Utrillo, *Rue Saint-Vincent, Montmartre,* 1930

Edgar Degas, *Café-Concert at the Ambassadeurs*, 1876-7

Lyon, France
GRENADINE PUNCH

1 6-ounce (170 gram) can frozen
    concentrated lemonade
1 6-ounce can frozen concentrated
    pineapple juice
1 6-ounce can frozen concentrated
    tangerine juice
½ cup French grenadine syrup
1 quart Perrier or soda water
1 orange, sliced
    Pineapple spears
    Lemon wedges
    Sprigs of fresh mint
    (last three optional)

Dilute lemonade according to directions on can. Pour mixture into ice-cube trays and freeze until hard.

Combine diluted pineapple juice, diluted tangerine juice and grenadine in a punch bowl. Stir until smooth and well blended. Slowly pour in Perrier or soda water and stir to blend.

Add lemonade ice cubes and float orange slices and, if desired, serve with pineapple spears or a lemon wedge and a sprig of fresh mint in each glass.
Serves: 8

Jerusalem, Israel
APPLE-WINE PUNCH

12 small apples, peeled and cored
1¼ cups sugar
1 teaspoon cinnamon
1 teaspoon chopped pecans
1½ cups orange juice
¼ cup tangerine syrup
    Juice of 1 lemon
2 cups dry red wine
1 cup tea

Fill the apple-core holes with 1 teaspoon of sugar each. Place apples in a baking dish and bake at 350° F. for 30 minutes.

Combine remaining sugar, cinnamon, pecans and the liquids. Heat over low heat (do not boil) for 15 minutes.

Place an apple in each of 12 individual punch cups and cover with the hot wine mixture.
Serves: 12

Tel Aviv, Israel
BRANDIED ORANGE PUNCH

6 cups orange juice
¾ cup sugar
6 cups strong tea
    Juice of 2 lemons
    Orange sections
    Cloves
1 cup peach brandy

Heat orange juice and sugar together. Combine with tea and lemon juice. Stud orange sections with cloves. Place in punch mixture. Stir in peach brandy, chill and serve.
Serves: 12

Paul Cézanne. *The Black Clock.* 1869-70

VERY HOT LEMON PUNCH

    5 lemons
    1 cup tea
    2 cups sugar
    1 nutmeg, crushed
    5 cups boiling water
    1 cup rum or cognac
    1 bottle dry red wine
      Lime slices
      Pineapple slices

Peel and squeeze lemons. Cook peels in the tea, sugar and nutmeg for 15 minutes. Add lemon juice. Strain resulting mixture into a large, heatproof container. Add boiling water, rum or cognac and wine. Let it settle for at least 15 minutes.

Serve very hot with slices of lime and pineapple.   *Serves: 6*

Boston, Massachusetts
POSSET ANGLAISE

    1 quart milk
    ⅓ cup sugar, or to taste
    2½ cups sherry
    1 cup heavy cream, whipped
      Grated nutmeg

Combine milk, sugar and sherry and heat until warm but not hot. Fold in whipped cream and sprinkle with nutmeg. May be served hot or cold.

(Posset Anglaise is a milk punch of the same family as eggnog, but less rich, less cloyingly sweet. Posset was originally a hot drink made with ale — as was eggnog, nog being a kind of strong ale from Norfolk, England — or with a strong white wine such as sherry.)

Serves: 12 (½ cup per serving)

Georges Braque, *Still-life*. 1932

London
LEMON-SPICE PUNCH

    1 cup sugar
    1 cinnamon stick
    5 whole cloves
    5 whole allspice
    2 cups water
    1 12-ounce can (340 grams) frozen
        lemonade concentrate
    1 12-ounce can frozen limeade concentrate
    2 large bottles quinine water
    2 large bottles carbonated water

Combine sugar, cinnamon, cloves, allspice and water in a small saucepan; heat to the boiling point and simmer 5 minutes. Strain and cool.

When ready to serve, pour spiced water into a punch bowl. Stir in frozen concentrates, quinine and carbonated waters.   *Serves: 15 to 20*

Munich, West Germany
CHAMPAGNE-PEACH PUNCH

    6 cups canned sliced peaches
    2 cups granulated sugar
    1 cup brandy
    1 bottle dry white wine
    1 magnum (2/5 gallon) champagne

Combine peaches, sugar and brandy in a large bowl. Mix carefully without crushing peaches. Chill in refrigerator for 24 hours.

Just before serving, add wine and champagne. Pour into a punch bowl and add only enough ice cubes to keep chilled. Float flowers on top for decoration, if desired.   *Serves: 12 to 15*

Paul Cézanne *The Card Players*, c. 1885-90

Hotel Andalucia Plaza, Marbella, Spain
WHITE SANGRIA

    1 fresh peach, sliced
    1 apple, sliced
    1 banana, sliced
    3 tablespoons Cointreau
    3 tablespoons cognac
    1 bottle white wine, cold
    1 cup soda water, cold
    Spiraled peel of 1 lemon

Marinate fruit slices in liqueur and brandy for 3 hours before serving. Combine with cold white wine and soda water in a pitcher. Garnish with spiraled lemon rind, removed in one piece.

Serves: 4 to 6

Luau Restaurant, Miami Beach, Florida
MAIDEN'S DOWNFALL

    1 tablespoon lime juice
    1½ tablespoons white rum
    1 cube canned pineapple
    1 tablespoon sugar syrup
    ½ tablespoon peach liqueur
    1-2 mint leaves, without stems
    Dash of bitters

Put all ingredients into blender. Mix until drink has consistency of loose sherbet. Pour into 6-ounce champagne glass. Garnish with mint leaf sprinkled with powdered sugar, if desired.

Serves: 1

Nicolas de Staël, *The Bottles*

Cork 'N Cleaver Restaurant, Colorado Springs, Colorado
HOT WINE ON A COLD NIGHT

    1 bottle red wine
    1 cup apple cider
    1 cup water
    1 cinnamon stick
    2 tablespoons sugar
    1 tablespoon lemon juice
    ½ teaspoon nutmeg
    3 cloves
    1 very generous dash of bitters

Boil ingredients together 15 minutes and strain. Serve hot.   *Serves: 4 to 6*

Grindelwald, Switzerland
GLUHWEIN

    4 bottles red wine
    1 cup sugar
    1 lemon, sliced
    4 oranges, sliced
    3 sticks cinnamon
    2 teaspoons cloves
    1 slice onion

Combine all ingredients in a large, heavy pot (not aluminum) and bring to a boil. Remove onion slice, cover and simmer for 20 minutes.

To serve, strain and reserve sliced fruit. Pour into punch bowl or individual glasses and float fruit slices. Serve while still hot.

Serves: 8 to 12

London
HOT BUTTERED RUM

1 cup brown sugar, firmly packed
¼ cup butter
½ teaspoon ground cinnamon
¼ teaspoon ground cloves
¼ teaspoon ground nutmeg
Hot water
3 tablespoons rum
Cinnamon sticks

Make a paste of the sugar, butter, ground cinnamon, cloves and nutmeg. Place a heaping tablespoon of the paste in bottom of each glass or mug. Add hot water to fill the glass ¾ full; stir well. Add 3 tablespoons rum to each glass, stir and add a cinnamon stick. Serve while hot.

Serves: 6 to 8

Richmond, Virginia
CITRUS WASSAIL

1 cup sugar
3 sticks cinnamon
12 cloves
¾ cup unsweetened orange juice
¼ cup unsweetened lemon juice
½ cup unsweetened grapefruit juice
2 cups apple cider
Maraschino cherries for garnish

Boil sugar and 2 cups water with cinnamon and cloves tied in a cheesecloth bag for 5 minutes. Remove spice bag and stir in citrus juices. Add apple cider and 4 cups water; bring to a boil. Serve warm, garnished with cherries.

Yield: 12 cups

Fresco of the triumphal arch, Calendar: *September*

DESSERT DRINKS

Velasquez, *Los Borrachos (The Triumph of Bacchus)*, 1629

Nottingham, England
WASSAIL WOOER

  1 gallon sweet or hard cider
10 sticks cinnamon
  1 tablespoon allspice
  ½ cup fresh-squeezed lemon juice
1½ cups sugar, or to taste
  1 bottle applejack of Calvados

Heat together all ingredients except applejack until mixture comes to a boil. Simmer for 15 minutes. Add applejack and serve hot in a punch bowl. The bowl may be decorated with slices of soft-roasted or baked apples, or with bite-size chunks of toasted French bread.

(The Middle English words *woes hoeil* mean ''be thou well'', a friendly and comforting toast when taking a drink in company. As with most traditional drinks, there are many recipes and many variations for the wassail bowl. Always a hot drink, it may be based on ale, wine or mulled sweet cider and spiced in different ways.)   *Serves: 25 (6 ounces per serving)*

Philadelphia, Pennsylvania
SHRUB OASIS

  1 pound (450 grams) sugar
  1 cup orange juice
2½ quarts rum

Dissolve sugar in orange juice. Add rum, mix well, cover and let stand 3 to 4 weeks. Strain and bottle. The flavor of orange peel may be added by soaking a few peelings in the rum for 12 hours. To serve, pour over shaved ice in a tall glass.

(The Arabic word for drink — *sharbah* — turns up in our words ''sherbet'' and ''shrub'', a drink with a fruit base. This is a slight modification of Benjamin Franklin's recipe for a shrub made with oranges and rum. Other shrubs use brandy and almost any fruit — cherries, peaches, plums, even tutti-frutti.)   *Serves: 15*

Vienna, Austria
CAFE VIENNA

> 2 cups strong coffee, freshly
>   brewed and hot
> Sugar
> Whipped cream

Pour coffee into tall cups and add sugar to taste. Top with whipped cream. In Vienna, practically everything is topped with whipped cream.

Serves: 2

Istanbul, Turkey
TURKISH COFFEE

> ¾ cup water
> 2 teaspoons sugar
> 2 tablespoons coffee, very finely ground

In a heavy saucepan, bring water and sugar to a boil. Add coffee and bring to a boil. Reduce heat and bring to a froth several times. Remove from heat and sprinkle in several drops of water.

To serve, spoon a little of the froth into 2 demitasse cups and then pour in the coffee.

In Turkey the froth is a sign of a good cup of coffee.

Serves: 2

Dublin, Ireland
IRISH COFFEE

> 4 teaspoons superfine sugar
> 1½ cups strong, hot coffee
> 4 tablespoons Irish whiskey
> Whipped cream

Warm 2 stemmed glasses and place 2 teaspoons sugar in the bottom of each. Fill to ⅔ full with hot coffee and stir well. Add 2 tablespoons Irish whiskey to each glass. Float whipped cream on top and serve immediately.

Serves: 2

Lausanne, Switzerland
CAFE DIABLO

> 6 regular-size cups espresso coffee
> 2 ounces (60 grams) Triple Sec liqueur
> 2 ounces Courvoisier brandy
> 1 ounce (30 grams) anise
> 12 cloves
>   Large orange rind
> 2 cinnamon sticks

First prepare the coffee espresso; have ready in a pot.

Pour liqueurs into a large silver bowl. Place bowl over flame or richaud and allow to heat for 1 minute. Flame the inside of the bowl with a match (liqueur will ignite). Have cloves prepared so you now have a long orange rind studded with cloves and twisted and held at one end by a fork. Hold rind about 2 feet above flaming bowl. Pick up liqueur with a ladle and gently let it run down the orange rind back into the bowl. Repeat this procedure 3 to 4 times. Now pour the coffee into the bowl, putting out the flame as you do so.

Serve in demitasse cups with pieces of cinnamon sticks in cups.

Serves: 8 to 12

Zürich, Switzerland
CAFE MOCHA

> 1 heaping tablespoon cocoa
> 1 cup hot milk
> 1 cup hot coffee
>   Whipped cream
>   Chocolate shavings for garnish

Combine cocoa and hot milk. Add coffee and heat, but do not boil. Pour into tall cups and top with whipped cream and chocolate shavings.

Serves: 2

Paul Cézanne, *Woman with Coffee Pot. c.* 1890

Auguste Renoir, *Place de la Trinité*, 1880-2

New York City
COFFEE DIABOLIUS

Spiraled peel of 1 large orange,
  removed in one piece
Whole cloves
1 cinnamon stick
2 heaping teaspoons sugar
6 tablespoons dark Jamaican rum
6 tablespoons cognac
2 cups hot double-strength coffee

Stud orange peel with cloves at approximately 2-inch intervals. Place cinnamon stick and sugar over heat in brûlot bowl (or chafing dish) and melt sugar, but do not burn. Add rum and continue heating mixture.

Fix one end of orange peel on a long, pronged fork and dip it in the mixture for a few seconds, mashing the peel slightly against the side of the bowl with the fork. Raise the orange peel so that one end slowly touches the liquid and, very slowly, dribble cognac down the orange peel. It will ignite along the entire peel and may continue to burn for 30 seconds or longer; cloves will turn bright amber. When flame has died out, return orange peel to the bowl. Add coffee and stir. Remove cinnamon stick.

Ladle steaming coffee into brûlot or demitasse cups. *Serves: 2*

Edouard Manet, *The Beer Waitress, c. 1878-9*

Monrovia, Liberia
GINGER BEER

25 pieces ginger
2 pineapples, unpeeled
2 teaspoons yeast (optional)
1 gallon boiling water
3½ cups molasses

Pulverize ginger. Add pineapple. Pour boiling water over this mixture (add yeast, if desired) and let stand overnight.

Next day strain, add molasses, chill and serve. (May be diluted with water if too strong. Extra sugar may be added, to taste.) *Serves: 10*

Paul Cézanne, *Bathers*

Honolulu, Hawaii
SAMOAN TYPHOON

½ cup fresh lime juice
¼ cup fresh orange juice
¼ cup pineapple juice
2 tablespoons honey
¼ cup passion fruit
½ cup Ron Rico dark rum
2 tablespoons Meyers rum
2 tablespoons 100-proof vodka
2 pineapple slices
2 sugared maraschino cherries

Combine all ingredients, except the garnish of pineapple slices and maraschino cherries, in a stainless-steel mixing cup over shaved ice. Chill. Then place in blender and mix for 30 seconds. Pour mix into large (21-ounce) brandy inhalers. Decorate with a pineapple slice and a sugared maraschino cherry.

Serves: 2

Monrovia, Liberia
GUAVA DRINK

Guava Juice

2 cups ripe guavas, fresh or canned
2 cups water

Wash guavas and take off blossom end. Slice and put slices into a pot; add enough water to cover. Boil quickly for 15 minutes. Remove from heat. Strain twice to remove all pulp and seeds. Put over heat again and bring to boiling point. Remove from heat and put in clean bottle and cool.

Conclusion

Guava Juice
¼ cup water
1-2 teaspoons sugar

Mix together. Chill and serve.

Serves: 2

Ocho Rios, Jamaica
PAWPAW DRINK

1 very ripe pawpaw
Water

Cut pawpaw in half. Remove seeds and peel. Mash well and sieve. Add water to mashed fruit (using equal quantities of pawpaw and water) and mix well.

Variations:

1. Add squeeze of lemon juice.
2. Use coconut water in place of water.
3. Add 1 teaspoon sugar per cup of water.
4. Add other mashed fruits or frozen juices.

Serves: 2

TART "INTERNATIONAL"

Cake

>   8 eggs
> 1½ cups sugar
>   2 cups cake flour
>   ½ cup butter, melted and cooled
> 1½ tablespoons cocoa
>   ½ cup almond meal (available in
>   some stores, or make your own from
>   blanched almonds in a blender)

Butter and flour three 8-inch springform cake pans. Have eggs at room temperature. In very large bowl begin beating eggs with an electric mixer. When foamy, add sugar and continue beating until mixture is very thick and forms a ribbon when beaters are lifted. Sift flour twice and add to batter in 3 parts. Fold in lightly. When almost all flour has been mixed in, pour in butter and mix very gently. Pour ⅓ of batter into a cake pan and set aside. Divide remaining batter in half. Sift cocoa into one portion; add almond meal to the other. Mix gently as before and pour into the other 2 pans.

Bake about 30 minutes at 350° F. Cool in pans for 10 minutes; then turn out on working surface and cool completely.

Filling

>   4 eggs
>   1 cup sugar
> 1½ cups unsalted butter, softened
>   1 teaspoon vanilla extract
>   ½ cup slivered almonds

Separate eggs. Reserve egg whites. Beat egg yolks with sugar until sugar dissolves and mixture is light yellow and somewhat thick. Put over hot, not boiling, water and cook, beating constantly. (A hand electric mixer makes this step easier.) Continue beating and cooking until mixture is very thick. It should form a broad ribbon when dropped from a spoon. This step will take about 20 minutes. Do not let water boil!

Pour egg-sugar custard into the large bowl of a stationary electric mixer. Let cool until comfortably to the touch. Start mixer at medium speed. When custard is just lukewarm, begin adding pieces of butter. Continue beating at high speed until custard is completely cold and all butter incorporated. Stir vanilla into cooled custard.

Beat egg whites until they form soft, shiny peaks. Do not overbeat. Put a large spoonful of egg whites into custard and mix thoroughly. Then pour custard mixture over egg whites and mix very gently. Filling should be very thick. It may be chilled for several hours to make it easier to handle. Stir in almonds just before assembling cake.

Icing

> 4 squares (4 ounces) dark semisweet
>   chocolate
> 3 tablespoons almond liqueur
> 4 tablespoons unsalted butter
>   Marzipan

Melt chocolate in liqueur in a double boiler. Add butter in small pieces. If icing is too soft, beat over iced water to thicken a bit. Reserve marzipan for garnishing finished cake.

Conclusion

Split cake layers with a long, sharp knife. Beginning with a cocoa layer, spread filling on each piece and stack, alternating cocoa, plain and almond layers. Frost cake with chocolate icing. Decorate with marzipan (the Hotel International uses its emblem; initials or a seasonal motif would be attractive at home). Store cake in the refrigerator if it is not to be used immediately. To serve, let stand at room temperature for about 20 minutes to let icing soften.

Serves: 16

Louisville, Kentucky
THE ORIGINAL KENTUCKY BOURBON CAKE

2 cups chopped candied
　　red cherries
1½ cups light seedless raisins
2 cups bourbon
1½ cups butter or margarine
2⅓ cups granulated sugar
2⅓ cups brown sugar, firmly packed
6 eggs, separated
5 cups sifted cake flour
4 cups shelled pecans
2 teaspoons nutmeg
1 teaspoon baking powder

Combine cherries, raisins and bourbon. Cover and let stand overnight.

Drain fruits; reserve bourbon. Cream butter or margarine and sugars together until light. Add egg yolks and beat well. Combine ½ cup of the flour and pecans. Sift together remaining flour, nutmeg and baking powder. Add flour mixture and reserved bourbon alternately to butter or margarine mixture, beating well after each addition. Beat egg whites until stiff but not dry. Fold egg whites into flour mixture. Fold soaked fruits and pecan-flour mixture into batter. Turn into greased 10-inch tube pan lined with greased waxed paper. Bake at 275° F. for 3½ hours. Cool. Remove from pan.

Fill center of cake with cheesecloth saturated with bourbon. Wrap in heavy waxed paper or aluminum foil. Store in tightly covered container in the refrigerator.　*Serves: 8 to 10*

The Tower Hotel, London
LIBERTY BELL

1 cup butter, unsalted
½ cup castor sugar
4 eggs, separated
½ pound (225 grams) unsweetened
　　chocolate, melted
　Sherry
2-pound (900-gram) pudding basin
1 small, round sponge cake
1 cup heavy cream

Cream together butter and sugar. Add egg yolks, one at a time. Stir in cooled melted chocolate. Whisk egg whites and fold in gently. Add sherry to taste.

Fill the bottom 3 inches of the pudding basin with the mixture. Slice sponge cake, lengthwise, into 3 layers and dampen with sherry. Place a layer, cut to fit basin, on top of pudding mixture. Add more mixture and repeat with sponge-cake layers until basin is filled. Refrigerate at least 1 hour.

Before serving, warm basin with hot water and turn out upside down, onto a serving plate. Whip the cream until very stiff and mound whipped cream on top of mold to obtain the shape of a bell.　*Serves: 8*

GATEAU GLACE AUX NOIX
(Iced Walnut Cake)

Sponge cake

   4 eggs
   ½ cup sugar
   1 teaspoon vanilla extract
   ¾ cup flour, sifted
   ½ cup butter, melted and cooled

Beat eggs and sugar together until mixture is light colored. Cook over hot, not boiling, water, beating constantly, until thick. This will take about 20 minutes. (An electric hand-mixer makes the process much easier.)

When the egg-sugar mixture is very thick, remove from heat. Add vanilla. Carefully fold in flour. When it has been incorporated, stir in melted butter.

Pour batter into a buttered and floured 8-inch cake pan and bake for 30 minutes at 350° F. When the cake is done, cool in the pan for 10 minutes; then turn out on working surface to cool completely.

Filling

   4 egg yolks
   ¾ cup sugar
   ⅔ cup milk, scalded
   1 cup cold, unsalted butter
   1 teaspoon vanilla extract

Beat egg yolks and sugar until mixture is thickened slightly and a light color. Beat in the hot milk in a very fine stream. Cook custard over hot, not boiling, water until it is thick enough to coat a spoon. Remove from heat; beat vigorously for a minute or two to cool somewhat. Cut the butter into small pieces. Add to custard, still beating constantly, a few pieces at a time, until all the butter is incorporated. The mixture should be thick and glossy. Stir in vanilla.

Conclusion

   ¼ cup kirsch
   2 cups tutti frutti ice cream
   1¼ cups walnuts

Split sponge cake into two layers. Sprinkle with kirsch. Assemble cake: a layer of sponge, a layer of filling, the ice cream, a layer of walnuts, another layer of filling, second layer of sponge. Frost the whole cake with the filling and decorate with walnuts. Put the cake in the freezer until 5 minutes before serving time.

Serves: 6

SWISS CHOCOLATE CAKE

Chocolate sponge

3 eggs
⅓ cup sugar
¼ cup flour
2 tablespoons cocoa
2 tablespoons butter, melted and cooled

Beat eggs and sugar until smooth; add flour, cocoa and butter. Mix gently but thoroughly. Turn into an 8-inch buttered cake pan and bake at 350° F. for about 18 minutes. The cake is done when it springs back from the touch and begins to pull away from the sides of the pan. Cool the sponge cake in the pan for 10 minutes. Remove and let cool thoroughly.

Filling

4 ounces (110 grams) malted chocolate
2 tablespoons rum
2 tablespoons butter
1 tablespoon dry instant coffee
½ cup heavy cream, whipped

Melt chocolate with rum and butter over hot, not boiling, water. Add coffee. Let mixture cool. Fold in whipped cream.

Frosting

4 ounces (110 grams) malted chocolate
2 tablespoons sugar
½ cup water

Melt chocolate over hot water. Add sugar and water. Beat over very cold water until frosting is of spreading consistency. If it hardens too much, beating over warm water will re-soften it.

Conclusion

Cut sponge cake into 3 layers. Spread filling between layers of cake and reassemble (a deep, springform pan is convenient). Chill the filled cake thoroughly. When cold, unmold cake and spread with frosting. *Serves: 8*

CHOCOLATE MOUSSE CAKE

Chocolate sponge cake

3 eggs
6 tablespoons sugar
½ cup sifted flour
¼ cup cocoa
2 tablespoons melted butter

Preheat oven to 350° F. Beat eggs, adding sugar a little at a time. Sift in flour and cocoa. Stir in melted butter. Mix until well blended. Pour into a 6-inch (2-inch-deep) round baking pan. Bake for 25 minutes at 350° F. Remove from oven and cool.

Mousse

4 egg whites
1 cup sugar
2 tablespoons unflavored gelatin,
    softened in a little cold water
¼ cup boiling water
3 squares (3 ounces) dark sweet chocolate
2 cups heavy cream, whipped

Beat together egg whites and 2 tablespoons of the sugar until mixture forms peaks. Using a candy thermometer, cook remaining sugar with 2 tablespoons of water in a saucepan until sugar is dissolved and temperature reaches 245° F. Beat the hot syrup into the meringue, pouring syrup in a thin stream. Dissolve softened gelatin in boiling water. Combine melted gelatin with egg-white mixture. Melt chocolate and add to mixture, blending thoroughly. Fold in whipped cream.

Slice the cake horizontally into 3 layers. Place 1 layer of cake in a circular mold, 6 inches in diameter. Then pour half of the mousse filling into the mold and repeat with another layer of cake and the balance of the mousse. Top with third layer of cake and chill for 30 minutes before frosting.

Chocolate icing

5 squares (5 ounces) dark sweet chocolate
¼ cup water

Melt chocolate and blend with water. Frost top of cake and chill again before serving.

Serves: 6

CHOCOLATE VELVET

Cake mold

1 basic sponge sheet, 11×16-inches
3 egg yolks
1 tablespoon instant coffee
¼ cup kirsch
¼ cup rum
¼ cup crème de cacao
⅓ cup firmly packed praline
  paste (can be bought in a can)
6 tablespoons melted butter
1½ pounds (675 grams) semisweet
  chocolate, melted
3 egg whites
  Pinch of salt
¼ cup confectioners' sugar
2 cups heavy cream, whipped
  (unsweetened)

Completely line a rounded 1-quart mold with basic sponge cake by cutting out a circle to fit the bottom of the mold. Then, from the remaining cake, cut 1 long or 2 short strips to cover the sides. Reserve any cake left over for the top.

Mix egg yolks, coffee, kirsch, rum, crème de cacao and praline paste. Beat until smooth. Add hot butter and hot melted chocolate. Beat egg whites with salt until they form soft peaks. Add sugar, a tablespoon at a time, beating well after each addition. Continue beating 5 more minutes, or until very stiff. Fold whipped cream and beaten egg whites into original mixture. Pour into the sponge-lined mold. Cover top with remaining sponge cake, fitting together any bits and pieces if there is not a single piece big enough. Place in refrigerator for 2 hours, or until filling is firm. To serve, loosen sides of mold with a sharp knife. Turn out upside-down onto a plate.

Semisweet chocolate icing

5 squares semisweet chocolate
¼ cup boiling water

Melt chocolate. Mix chocolate and water, blending well. Frost cake all over and chill.

Serves: 8

Atlanta, Georgia

CANDY CRUNCH CAKE

Candy crunch preparation (day before)

1 pint corn syrup
¼ cup sugar
Pinch of baking soda

Put syrup and sugar in double boiler until mixture turns brown. Add baking soda. The mixture should begin to rise in 30 seconds. Remove from heat and pour into open pan. Let harden for 24 hours. While cake is baking, break into pieces and crush with a rolling pin.

1 pint heavy cream
1 cup custard

Whip heavy cream and store in refrigerator for 24 hours.

Prepare custard (any recipe) 24 hours in advance and store in refrigerator.

Cake preparation (day of use)

1½ cups egg whites (about 9)
1 teaspoon cream of tartar
1⅓ cups sugar
1⅓ cups sifted cake flour
1 teaspoon salt
⅔ cup egg yolks (about 5)
Raspberry jelly

Beat egg whites until firm. Add cream of tartar and beat until firm again. Gradually add sugar and beat mixture until stiff and glossy. Fold sifted flour and salt into whites and mix thoroughly. Fold in egg yolks and mix well.

Pour into 10-inch greased pan. Bake at 325° F. in a preheated oven for about 1¼ hours. When done, invert cake on rack until cool.

When cake is cool, place on flat surface and even off top and bottom with a long knife. Cut cake in half.

On bottom half spread a thin layer of jelly. Spread generous layer of custard on top of jelly. Place top half of cake on top of custard. *Do not press down.* Spread whipped cream generously on sides and top of cake with a 1-inch spatula. Sprinkle crunch on whipped cream by handfuls to completely cover. Place in refrigerator until ready to serve.

Note: Cake will melt in 3 to 4 hours because of moisture in refrigerator.

Serves: 8

SCHWARTZWALD TORTE
(Black Forest Cake)

Torte

6 eggs, separated
¾ cup sifted flour
¼ cup sifted cocoa
¼ teaspoon salt
1¼ cups sugar
1 teaspoon vanilla extract

Separate yolks from whites of eggs and allow both to warm to room temperature. Meanwhile, sift flour once, measure, add cocoa and salt and sift again. In small bowl of electric mixer, beat egg yolks until thick and lemon-colored. Add ¾ cup of the sugar gradually and continue to beat until entire mixture is thick and creamy. Transfer to large mixer bowl. Beat egg whites until frothy throughout, then add remaining ½ cup sugar gradually, beating constantly. Continue to beat until stiff peaks form. Fold into egg-yolk mixture. Sift flour mixture gradually over egg mixture, folding gently but thoroughly. Add vanilla and blend. Turn into 2 deep 9-inch layer-cake pans, the bottoms of which have been lightly greased and floured. Bake at 350° F. about 25 minutes, or until cake tests done. Remove from oven and cool in pans 10 minutes.

Brandy glaze

¼ cup sugar
1 tablespoon water
¼ cup brandy

To make a glaze, combine the sugar and water in small saucepan. Place over low heat and stir until sugar is dissolved. Remove from heat and cool slightly, then add brandy. Cut cake layers from sides of pans and remove to wire cake racks. Brush brandy glaze over top of warm layers and allow to cool.

Frosting and garnish

2 cups heavy cream
¼ cup confectioners' sugar
2 tablespoons brandy
Shaved chocolate
Maraschino cherries

To make frosting, combine cream and confectioners' sugar and chill thoroughly. Beat until thick and light, then add brandy. Spread whipped-cream frosting on 1 layer of cake and top with the second layer. Use remainder of cream to frost sides and top. Sprinkle with shaved chocolate and garnish with well-drained maraschino cherries. Keep refrigerated.

Serves: 6 to 8

BROWN DERBY GRAPEFRUIT CAKE

Cake

1½ cups sifted cake flour
¾ cup sugar
1½ teaspoons baking powder
½ teaspoon salt
¼ cup water
¼ cup vegetable oil
3 eggs, separated
⅜ tablespoon grapefruit juice
½ teaspoon grated lemon rind
¼ teaspoon cream of tartar

Sift together flour, sugar, baking powder and salt into mixing bowl. Make a well in center of dry ingredients and add water, oil, egg yolks, grapefruit juice and lemon rind. Beat until very smooth. Beat egg whites and cream of tartar separately until whites are stiff but not dry. Gradually pour egg yolk mixture over whites, folding gently with a rubber spatula until just blended. *Do not stir* mixture.

Pour into an ungreased 9-inch cake pan. Bake at 350° F. for 25 to 30 minutes, or until cake springs back when lightly touched with finger. Invert pan on cake rack until cool. Run spatula around edge of cake and carefully remove from pan. With a serrated knife, gently cut layer in half.

Grapefruit cream-cheese frosting

¾ pound (340 grams) cream cheese
2 teaspoons lemon juice
1 teaspoon grated lemon rind
¾ cup powdered sugar, sifted
1 1-pound can (450 grams) grapefruit
    sections, well drained
6-8 drops yellow food coloring

Let cream cheese soften at room temperature. Beat cheese until fluffy. Add lemon juice and rind. Gradually blend in sugar. Beat until well blended. Crush broken grapefruit sections to measure 2 teaspoons. Blend into frosting. Stir in food coloring. Spread frosting on bottom half of cake. Top with several grapefruit sections. Cover with second layer. Frost top and sides and garnish with remaining grapefruit sections.
Serves: 8

PAN DI SPAGNA
(Italian Rum Cake)

Cake

1 tablespoon soft butter
½ cup warm milk
2 eggs, separated
1 cup sugar
1 teaspoon baking powder
1 cup flour

Combine soft butter and warm milk and set aside. In a small mixing bowl place egg yolks and ½ cup of the sugar; in a large mixing bowl place egg whites and the rest of the sugar. With an electric mixer at medium speed, beat egg yolks and sugar until mixture is pale yellow. Set aside. Wash and dry beaters of the mixer. Set at highest speed and beat egg yolks into egg whites. Reduce speed to medium and mix for 5 minutes. Gradually add the milk-butter mixture. Sift baking powder and flour together. Reduce mixer speed to low and gradually incorporate flour. Mix until smooth.

Pour batter into a greased 9-inch cake pan and place immediately in a preheated 350° F. oven. Baking should take 30 minutes, but use a cake tester to make sure the layer is done. Place a 24-inch sheet of aluminum foil on a flat surface. Invert cake pan over it until it is completely cool.

Cream filling

3 tablespoons sugar
2 cups milk
3 tablespoons cornstarch
1 teaspoon vanilla extract

Mix sugar, milk, cornstarch and vanilla in a saucepan with an electric beater until well blended. Cook over low heat, stirring constantly. When mixture comes to a boil, remove from heat. Stir vigorously until it is cool.

Conclusion

½ cup rum
¼ cup toasted almonds

Cut cake horizontally into 3 layers. Place bottom layer on a cake platter and spoon some rum over it. Spread evenly about ⅓-inch of custard over the layer. Cover with second layer of cake and repeat process until all 3 layers are used. Spread remaining custard over top and sides of cake and sprinkle with chopped almonds. Refrigerate at least 1 hour before serving. *Serves: 12*

PARIS BRESSE
(Cream-Filled Pastry Ring)

Pâte à Chou

¼ cup butter
½ cup water
½ cup flour
4 eggs
¼ cup slivered almonds

Boil butter and water together. When butter is melted, add all flour at once and beat until smooth. Beat in eggs one at a time, continuing to beat until mixture is smooth and creamy. Lightly butter a 12-inch round, heatproof tray. Put Pâte à Chou into a pastry bag and pipe around edge of tray, forming a thick ring of pastry. Sprinkle with almonds and bake at 400° F. for 20 minutes.

Crème Pâtissière

3 egg yolks
½ cup sugar
¼ cup flour
1¼ cups milk
¼ teaspoon vanilla extract

Beat egg yolks until light. Gradually add sugar and beat until mixture forms a ribbon when lifted from beater. Add flour and blend thoroughly. In a separate saucepan, boil milk and vanilla together. Add half of the vanilla-milk to batter and stir rapidly. Return this mixture to remaining milk and bring to a boil, beating rapidly and continuously until well-blended.

Crème Chantilly

1¼ cups heavy cream
2 tablespoons sugar
½ teaspoon vanilla extract

Beat cream and sugar together until mixture is fluffy. Add vanilla.

Conclusion

½ cup whole strawberries
6 pineapple-ring halves
Powdered sugar

Cut pastry ring in half, horizontally. Place bottom half on a serving dish. Mix half of the Crème Pâtissière with half of the Crème Chantilly. Place this in a pastry bag. Pipe onto lower half of ring. Place top half of ring on bottom half. Refill pastry bag with remaining Crème Pâtissière and Crème Chantilly. Pipe ten rosettes around top of ring. Decorate with whole strawberries placed on each rosette and pineapple slices between rosettes. Sprinkle powdered sugar over all.

Serves: 6

LE CROQUEMBOUCHE
(Pastry Tower)

Filled pastry

> 1 cup butter
> 1 cup water
>   Pinch of salt
>   Pinch of sugar
> 1½ cups flour
> 8 eggs
> ½ cup heavy cream, whipped
> 2 tablespoons rum

Bring butter, water, salt and sugar to a boil. Add flour at once, stirring briskly, and remove from heat. Beat until batter forms a ball. Add eggs, one at a time, beating well after each addition. Pipe from a pastry bag onto an ungreased baking sheet to form small puffs.

Bake at 400° F. until golden and puffed. Slit and remove soft centers; turn off oven and return puffs to dry out a few minutes. Combine whipped cream with rum. When puffs are cool, fill with the flavored whipped cream.

Nougatine

> 2 cups sugar
> ¾ cup water
> 2 cups chopped almonds
> 1 teaspoon salad (not olive) oil

Cook sugar and water until a very thick, dark syrup is formed. Add almonds and pour onto a cold slab of oiled marble or metal. When cool enough to handle, reserve a small portion and shape the rest into a cone. Make several fancy shapes — stars or flowers — from the reserved nougatine.

Caramel

> 1¼ cups sugar
> ½ cup water

Boil sugar and water together until a thick, dark syrup forms.

Conclusion

Place cooled nougatine cone, large end down, on a large platter. One by one dip filled puffs in caramel syrup (reheat if it gets too stiff) and place around nougatine close to each other, round sides out, to build a pyramid. Finally, decorate with pieces of shaped nougatine. Assemble croquembouche as near as possible to serving time since cream-filled puffs are very, very perishable and refrigeration would spoil texture of the puffs.   *Serves: 8*

CREAM SANDWICH

Puff Pastry Dough

4½ cups white flour
½ cup butter
½ teaspoon salt
1 cup water
Dash of lemon juice
2 cups butter

Form a well in flour. In the well mix ½ cup butter, salt, lemon juice and water. Add flour gradually and work to a firm dough. Shape into a ball, cut a cross in the top and let rest in a cool place for 1 hour.

Roll out in a square about ⅛-inch thick. Knead 2 cups butter until soft enough to shape into a square. Place in center of dough square. Press lightly to flatten. Place on a cloth dusted with flour and let rest in a cool place for about 15 minutes. Roll out to about a 12-inch rectangle and fold in thirds. Repeat this operation 6 times, rolling the dough from a different side each time and letting it rest about 15 minutes between each operation.

Vanilla Cream

5 egg yolks
¾ cup sugar
1 teaspoon vanilla extract
1 cup milk
½ vanilla bean

Beat egg yolks, sugar and vanilla extract together until slightly foamy. Bring milk to a boil with vanilla bean. Pour boiling milk very slowly into egg mixture, stirring constantly. Return to saucepan. Stir cream over low heat until thick enough to coat a wooden spoon. Remove from heat and stir until cool. Strain.

Conclusion

Puff Pastry Dough
2 cups Vanilla Cream
3 cups heavy cream, whipped
1½ cups sugar
5 tablespoons kirsch

Divide dough into 3 strips, 8 inches long and 6 inches wide. Place them on a cookie sheet and bake for 5 minutes at 350° F. Mix Vanilla Cream with 1 cup whipped cream and 1 tablespoon kirsch and coat one strip of pastry. Cover with a second strip of pastry and coat that with 2 cups whipped cream, which has been mixed with ¾ cup sugar and 1 tablespoon kirsch. Place third strip of pastry on top and glaze with icing which has been made with ¾ cup sugar and remaining kirsch.

Serves: 4 to 6

YOGURT PASTRY WITH SYRUP

3 cups water
3½ cups sugar
3 eggs
1 cup flour
1 teaspoon baking powder
1 cup yogurt
1 teaspoon grated lemon or orange rind
1 teaspoon lemon juice
Whipped cream

Mix water with 2½ cups of the sugar. Boil until it forms a syrup. Set aside to cool. To make a pastry, beat eggs into remaining sugar until sugar is dissolved. Sift flour with baking powder. Add yogurt, sifted flour, grated rind and lemon juice to egg mixture and beat until smooth.

Grease a 9-inch square baking pan well, pour pastry mixture into it and bake at 400° F. for 30 minutes. After removing from oven, leave pastry in the pan and cut into diamond shapes. Pour cold syrup over pastry. Leave pan uncovered until all syrup has been absorbed by pastry. When cool, chill in refrigerator. Garnish with whipped cream before serving.

Serves: 8

Jerusalem, Israel
BASBOUSA
(Sweet Rum Loaf)

5 cups sugar
2 cups margarine, melted
½ teaspoon salt
5 pounds (2¼ kilograms) semolina
Warm water
1 teaspoon vanilla extract
½ teaspoon almond extract

Combine sugar and margarine. Add salt, semolina and enough warm water to make a soft dough. Add vanilla and almond extract and knead thoroughly.

Place dough in a greased, square baking tin. Bake at 350° F. until the top is golden. While loaf is baking, prepare syrup (below).

When loaf is done, remove from oven and cut into squares immediately. Place squares in individual dessert bowls and cover with syrup. Serve at once.

Syrup

2 cups sugar
1 cup water
1 tablespoon lemon juice
¼ cup rum

Bring sugar and water to a boil. Add lemon juice and cook, stirring constantly, until mixture thickens. Remove from heat, cool and add rum.

Serves: 8

OM ALY

Pastry

3 cups flour
2 egg yolks
4 tablespoons butter
½ teaspoon salt
¾ cup water
4 cups clarified butter

Mix flour, egg yolks, butter, salt and water. Work paste until soft. Cut into egg-size pieces. Cover with a wet napkin and let rest for 30 minutes.

Roll out thinly on an oiled marble table. Fry pieces of dough individually in browned butter.

Conclusion

8 cups milk
8 cups sugar
2 teaspoons vanilla extract
1 pound (450 grams) almonds
½ pound (225 grams) pistachios
½ pound walnuts
1 pound raisins
2½ cups Crème Chantilly (see p. 172)

Heat milk to boiling with sugar and vanilla. Lay fried pastry in a baking dish, then cover with a layer of nuts and raisins. Repeat to fill the dish. Add boiling milk and let stand for 5 minutes until platter is soaked with milk. Cover with Crème Chantilly.

Place dish in 400° F. oven until top is brown, about 15 minutes. Serve hot.   *Serves: 12*

"CLARE DE LUNE" AVEC SAUCE AUX MURES DE BOIS

2 tablespoons raisins
2 tablespoons kirsch
2 tablespoons soft marzipan
1 scoop French-vanilla ice cream
2 egg whites
2 teaspoons sugar
1 round slice almond-flavored sponge
    or pound cake
  Blackberry sauce (optional)

Soak raisins in kirsch for several hours or overnight.

Drain and mix raisins with marzipan. Form marzipan into a ball. Slightly soften ice cream; wrap it around marzipan to form a larger ball. Return to freezer until *very* hard.

When ready to serve, preheat oven to 500° F. Beat egg whites to form a stiff, shiny meringue. Place cake round on a wooden cutting board; place ice cream-marzipan ball on top of cake and quickly cover ice cream completely with meringue to form "la lune". Brown only a minute or two in oven. Serve immediately. If desired, serve blackberry sauce separately.

Serves: 1

MIRABELLE SURPRISE DES CORDELIERS

Macaroons

½ cup blanched almonds
1 cup sugar
2 egg whites
2 tablespoons sugar
2 tablespoons light corn syrup

Grind together almonds and 1 cup sugar. Add egg whites and grind again. In a saucepan cook the 2 tablespoons sugar and syrup until it forms a large ball. Add the sugar-almond-egg mixture. Place batter in a pastry bag and squeeze out little round macaroons on moistened paper.

Bake at 250° F. until dry and lightly browned.

Ice Cream

1 cup Mirabelle plums (small French plums also available canned)
½ cup plum brandy
4 cups milk
6 egg yolks
1¼ cups sugar

Soak plums in plum brandy for several hours.

After soaking, drain plums, reserving the brandy. Mix milk, egg yolks and sugar. To avoid crushing plums, add them when the mixture has been almost entirely blended. Pour ice-cream mixture into a round mold, placing macaroons on top. Freeze until very firm.

Meringue

8 egg whites
4½ cups sugar
2½ cups almonds, crushed

Beat egg whites until frothy; add sugar and continue beating until very stiff. Sift almonds and blend in.

Conclusion

½ cup chopped almonds
¼ cup sugar

Unmold ice cream onto a round serving dish. Over it pipe the meringue, using a pastry bag. Sprinkle chopped almonds over it and sugar to glaze. Place under broiler until lightly caramelized. Flame with reserved plum brandy.

Serves: 10

COURONNE D'ANANAS MARIETTE

Crown of Pineapple

1 large fresh pineapple
3 fresh peaches, peeled and halved
  Glazing Syrup (below)
½ cup orange sherbet
½ cup lemon sherbet
1 cup praline ice cream
½ cup fresh raspberries
½ cup fresh strawberries
  Meringue à la Swiss (below)
  Langues de Chat (below)

Cup pineapple lengthwise. Scoop out the flesh, chop and set aside. Glaze the pineapple half-shells and peach halves with Glazing Syrup and chill.

Fill chilled half-shells with scoops of the sherbets and ice cream and then with the chopped pineapple, the raspberries and strawberries.

Cover with Meringue à la Swiss. Garnish with chilled, glazed peach halves and stud with Langues de Chat to resemble a crown.

Glazing Syrup

1 cup sugar
⅓ cup water

Boil sugar and water together until a little beyond the soft ball stage — 244° F. on a candy thermometer. Coat peaches and pineapple shells with the glaze and refrigerate until thoroughly chilled.

Meringue à la Swiss

4 egg whites
1 cup powdered sugar
1 tablespoon crème de menthe

In the top of a double boiler, over boiling water, beat egg whites and powdered sugar until stiff. Slowly beat in crème de menthe.

Langues de Chat

¼ cup butter, softened
⅓ cup sugar
1 lemon peel, grated
2-3 egg whites (¼ cup)
⅓ cup flour

Beat together butter, sugar and grated peel in a mixing bowl. When pale and fluffy, pour in egg whites and blend lightly. Gradually sift and stir in flour.

Lightly butter and dust with flour 2 baking sheets. Using a saucer or other round object, mark off 4 circles (about 5½ inches in diameter) on each sheet. Lightly oil 2 large cups or small bowls (about 4 inches in diameter at the top, 2 inches at the bottom and 2½ inches deep). Set aside.

Place a tablespoon of batter into each circle on the cookie sheets and spread to about 1/16-inch thickness. Bake at 450° F. for 5 minutes, or until cookies have browned lightly to within about an inch of their centers.

To avoid cookies becoming too crisp to work with, bake one sheet of cookies at a time. Working with one cookie at a time, remove cookie with a flexible spatula and turn over an oiled cup. With your fingers, press cookie against sides and bottom of cup. Repeat procedure with each cookie, removing crisped cookies from cup after each initial step.

This batter makes eight 3½-inch Langues de Chat. They can be frozen and kept indefinitely.

Serves: 4 to 6

STRAWBERRY HUGHES

6 ounces (170 grams) fresh strawberries
Drambuie
Strawberry jelly
8 ounces (225 grams) butter
8 ounces crushed digestive biscuits
½ cup heavy cream

Wash, stem and halve the strawberries. Marinate in a little Drambuie for at least 1 hour.

Line the bottom of a fluted savarin ring mold with a little strawberry jelly. When almost set, decorate with marinated strawberry halves. Allow to set completely.

Prepare the fruit bavaroise. When cooled, fill the mold half full and place in a bowl of crushed ice to set quickly.

Prepare filling. Place a little of the filling on top of the mold, then fill to ¼-inch from the top with the remaining fruit bavaroise. Allow to set.

Melt butter and add crushed biscuits; cool. Fill the top of the mold with the biscuit base. Chill in refrigerator until ready to serve.

Turn out mold by warming in hot water. Fill the center with remaining filling and decorate with whipped cream.

Fruit Bavaroise

1 cup fresh strawberry purée
6 tablespoons castor sugar
2 tablespoons gelatine
Drambuie
3 drops red food coloring
2 cups heavy cream
3 egg whites

Put strawberry purée, sugar, gelatin and a little Drambuie in a bowl and place over hot water until gelatin is dissolved. Add food coloring. Cool.

Filling

2 cups red wine
1 cup strawberry preserves
6 ounces (170 grams) fresh strawberries, washed, stemmed and halved
1 tablespoon cornstarch (approximate)
Sugar to taste

In a saucepan heat wine and reduce by half. Blend in preserves and cook to form a very thick sauce. Carefully stir in strawberries. Add cornstarch to bind. Sweeten with sugar to taste.

Serves: 8

Restaurant Gundel, Budapest, Hungary

SOMLO DUMPLINGS

Walnut dough

¼ cup sugar
½ cup flour
¼ cup ground walnuts
3 eggs
2 tablespoons crème de cacao

Sift sugar and flour together. Mix in ground walnuts. Beat eggs. Stir in crème de cacao. Add to dry ingredients.

Form dough into 6 ladyfinger-shaped cookies and bake on a greased cookie sheet at 200° F. until dry — about 30 minutes. Let cool completely.

Filling

½ cup milk
1 tablespoon flour
2 tablespoons vanilla sugar
3 tablespoons sugar
1 egg

Heat milk to scalding. Mix flour into sugars. Beat egg and add sugar mixture. Beat a little of the hot milk into egg mixture; then add to milk. Cook over hot, not boiling, water until custard thickens to the consistency of mayonnaise. Cool.

Chocolate icing

3 tablespoons sugar
2 tablespoons water
1½ tablespoons crème de cacao
1 tablespoon rum

Boil sugar and water together to form a fairly heavy syrup; cool slightly and add crème de cacao and rum. Cool completely before using.

Conclusion

¼ cup dark rum
¼ cup water
2 tablespoons finely chopped raisins
2 tablespoons finely chopped walnuts
½ cup heavy cream, whipped

Moisten walnut cookies with mixture of rum and water. Sprinkle with finely chopped raisins and walnuts. Spread prepared, cooled filling on cookies and refrigerate.

At serving time, place each cookie on a small plate. Dribble prepared chocolate icing over each one and decorate with unsweetened whipped cream.

Serves: 6

AVOCADO CREAM IN FROSTED ORANGE SHELLS

  2 large navel oranges
  ½ egg whites, slightly beaten
  ½ cup confectioners' sugar
  ½ teaspoon unflavored gelatin
  1 small avocado (about 3 ounces, or
      90 grams)
    Crushed ice
    Mint sprigs

Cut a 1-inch-thick slice from top of each orange. Also cut just enough from bottom of each so orange will stand upright. Holding oranges over a bowl to collect juice, carefully scoop orange pulp out of shells. Drain juice from shells into measuring cup; set aside ½ cup of juice. Cut orange pulp into bite-size pieces; measure 1 cup. Refrigerate. Brush rim and outside of orange shells with egg white. Place ¼ cup of the sugar on waxed paper and roll the shells in it to coat well. Place on wire rack; refrigerate.

Sprinkle gelatin over reserved orange juice; let stand 5 minutes, to soften. Set over hot water; stir until dissolved.

Halve avocado, remove pit and peel. Place avocado in electric-blender container with remaining sugar and the gelatin mixture. Blend avocado mixture at high speed until smooth. Refrigerate, covered, just until set — about 2 hours.

To serve, place frosted orange shells in crushed ice in dessert dishes. Divide orange pieces into shells, reserving 6 orange sections for garnish. Beat avocado cream with a wooden spoon until smooth. Mound in orange shells. Decorate with reserved orange pieces and mint sprigs.

Serves: 2

ZABAGLIONE WITH CHANTILLY CREAM

  2 teaspoons unflavored gelatin
  3 tablespoons cold water
  9 large egg yolks
  9 tablespoons sugar
  1 cup Marsala wine
    Chantilly cream (below)
  6 glacé cherries
    Unsweetened chocolate

Soften gelatin in cold water and melt in double boiler. Whip egg yolks in another double boiler and slowly whip in sugar and wine. Beat vigorously until mixture is foamy and starting to thicken. Add softened gelatin and continue beating while taking mixture away from heat. Pour into custard cups and chill.

Just before serving, garnish each portion with dollop of Chantilly cream, a glacé cherry and a few shavings of chocolate.

Chantilly cream

  1 cup heavy cream
  2 tablespoons confectioners' sugar
  ½ teaspoon vanilla extract

Whip heavy cream, not too stiff. Fold in sugar and vanilla gently, but thoroughly.

Serves: 6

San Francisco, California
BOURBON BALLS

1½ cups finely crushed vanilla wafers
½ cup confectioners' sugar
¾ tablespoon cocoa
¾ cup finely chopped California walnuts
1½ tablespoon corn syrup
¼ cup bourbon
Granulated or confectioners' sugar

Mix together crushed wafer crumbs, confectioners' sugar, cocoa, walnuts, corn syrup and bourbon. Mix well and shape into 1-inch balls. Roll in granulated or confectioners' sugar. Store in container with tight-fitting lid.

Yield: 1½ dozen

San Francisco, California
BOURBON FUDGE BALLS

½ cup finely crushed vanilla wafers
2 tablespoons bourbon
¼ cup semisweet chocolate morsels
⅛ cup sweetened, condensed milk
Sweet milk cocoa or finely chopped California walnuts

Combine crushed wafer crumbs and bourbon; mix until crumbs are moistened. In a double boiler, melt chocolate over hot (not boiling) water. Add condensed milk and stir just to blend. Gradually stir chocolate mixture into crumb mixture.

Shape into 1-inch balls. Roll in sweet milk cocoa or walnuts. Let stand until cool.

Yield: 2 dozen

Dar Es Salaam, Tanzania
KASHATA
(Coconut Balls)

¼ pound (110 grams) sugar
½ teaspoon cinnamon
1 coconut, grated (1 cup)

Melt sugar and add cinnamon and grated coconut. Cook in shallow pan, stirring occasionally, until sugar turns light brown and begins to set. (A good test: Put a drop of water in the pan when sugar begins to turn brown; when this drop sets into a fairly hard ball, remove pan from heat.)

When mixture is cool but still soft, form into egg-size balls and leave to set.   *Serves: 4*

Columbia, South Carolina
PRALINES

2 cups sugar
1 cup brown sugar, firmly packed
3 tablespoons light corn syrup
¾ cup evaporated milk
½ cup water
2 teaspoons maple flavoring
1 cup pecans, roughly chopped
Pecan halves

Combine all ingredients except chopped pecans and pecan halves. Cook mixture to 236° F. on a candy thermometer; remove from heat and cool. Add chopped pecans and beat until mixture becomes stiff.

Quickly drop spoonfuls onto a well-buttered sheet. Patties should be about 4 inches in diameter. Press one or more pecan halves on top of each patty. Work quickly as pralines will become stiff very quickly. Place between sheets of waxed paper.　*Yield: 1 dozen*

Linz, Austria
ZWETSCHKENWURST
(Prune Sausage Confection)

½ pound (225 grams) prunes
¼ cup water
1 cup sugar
⅛ pound (55 grams) figs, dried, diced
1 cup chopped walnuts
¼ cup sugar

Wash prunes; simmer in water to cover for 15 minutes. Drain, pit and chop. Boil water with sugar until it forms a soft ball when dropped in cold water. Add prunes and cook to a thick purée — about 30 minutes. Add figs and nuts.

Sprinkle a board with sugar. Place mixture on top and roll into sausage shape. Let dry. Cut into thin slices before serving.　*Serves: 6*

Jerusalem, Israel
PUMPKIN AND RICE JAM

½ cup brown sugar
1 pound (450 grams) pumpkin, peeled and finely grated
2 cups orange juice
1½ cups rice, uncooked
½ teaspoon salt
Pinch of nutmeg
½ cup dry figs, thinly sliced
½ cup dates, pitted and thinly sliced
¼ cup currants
Peel of 1 orange, grated
Sour cream
Cinnamon

Melt sugar over low heat in a little water, stirring constantly to prevent burning. Add pumpkin. Cover and cook slowly for 30 minutes. Add orange juice. Bring mixture to a boil and stir in rice, salt and nutmeg. Add figs, dates, currants and orange peel and cook for an additional 30 minutes.

If desired, accompany with sour cream sprinkled with cinnamon.　*Serves: 4*

Edinburgh, Scotland
BUTTER-CREAM FROSTING

¼ cup butter
2 cups powdered sugar
1½ teaspoons vanilla extract
½ teaspoon almond extract
3 tablespoons light cream

Cream butter, gradually adding 1 cup of the powdered sugar. Add vanilla and almond extract and beat well. Add cream alternately with remaining sugar until mixture is of spreading consistency.   *Yield: 1½ cups*

New York City
CHOCOLATE GLAZE

6 ounces (170 grams) semisweet
   chocolate morsels
2 tablespoons butter
2 tablespoons light corn syrup
2 tablespoons hot water

In the top of a double boiler over hot (not boiling) water, melt chocolate with butter, corn syrup and water. Stir to blend well.

With a spatula, spread glaze over top of cake, letting some run down side of cake.

Allow cake to stand about 1 hour, or until glaze is firm enough to cut.   *Yield: ¾ cup*

New York City
BOURBON GLAZE

¼ cup butter
½ cup bourbon
⅔ cup confectioners' sugar

Combine all ingredients and heat until sugar is completely dissolved.   *Yield: 1 cup*

Zürich, Switzerland
VELVET CHOCOLATE SAUCE

4 squares (4 ounces) semisweet chocolate
¾ cup sugar
¾ cup undiluted evaporated milk
⅛ teaspoon salt
½ teaspoon vanilla extract
1½ teaspoons dark rum (optional)

In the top of a double boiler, melt chocolate. Stir in sugar. Cover and cook over simmering water for 15 minutes, stirring occasionally. Stir in remaining ingredients. Cover and keep over warm water until ready to serve. (Can be stored in refrigerator and reheated.)
              Yield: 1½ cups

Masson's Restaurant Français, New Orleans, Louisiana
SABAYON

6 eggs, separated
¾ cup granulated sugar
¾ cup cream sherry wine
¾ cup heavy cream, whipped
1 teaspoon vanilla extract

Beat egg yolks with sugar until creamy. Add sherry and cook in double boiler until thick. Cool in mixing bowl for 10 to 15 minutes. Add whipped cream. Beat egg whites with vanilla until stiff; fold into mixture. Chill for 2 to 3 hours.   *Serves: 6*

LIQUID MEASURES:

1 dash	= 6 drops
1 teaspoon	= ⅓ tablespoon
1 tablespoon	= 3 teaspoons
1 tablespoon	= ½ fluid ounce
1 fluid ounce	= 2 tablespoons
1 jigger	= 3 tablespoons
1 jigger	= 1½ fluid ounces
1 cup	= ½ pint
1 cup	= 16 tablespoons
1 cup	= 8 fluid ounces
1 pint	= 2 cups
1 pint	= 16 fluid ounces
1 fifth	= 25 fluid ounces
1 quart	= 2 pints
1 quart	= 4 cups
1 quart	= 32 fluid ounces
1 gallon	= 4 quarts
1 gallon	= 16 cups
1 gallon	= 128 fluid ounces

DRY MEASURES:

1 dash	= less than ⅛ teaspoon
1 teaspoon	= ⅓ tablespoon
1 tablespoon	= 3 teaspoons
¼ cup	= 4 tablespoons
⅓ cup	= 5 tablespoons plus 1 teaspoon
½ cup	= 8 tablespoons
⅔ cup	= 10 tablespoons plus 2 teaspoons
¾ cup	= 12 tablespoons
⅞ cup	= 14 tablespoons
1 cup	= 16 tablespoons
1 pint	= 2 cups
1 quart	= 4 cups
1 peck	= 8 cups
1 bushel	= 4 pecks

AVOIRDUPOIS WEIGHT:

1 ounce	= 28 grams*
¼ pound	= 4 ounces (110 grams)
½ pound	= 8 ounces (225 grams)
1 pound	= 16 ounces (450 grams)

OVEN TEMPERATURES:

		Fahrenheit:	Centigrade:
Very slow oven	=	250 - 275 F.	121 - 135 C.
Slow oven	=	300 - 325 F.	149 - 163 C.
Moderate oven	=	350 - 375 F.	177 - 191 C.
Hot oven	=	400 - 425 F.	204 - 218 C.
Very hot oven	=	450 - 475 F.	232 - 246 C.
Extemely hot oven	=	500 - 525 F.	260 - 274 C.

CONFECTION TEMPERATURES:

		Fahrenheit:	Centigrade:**
Jellying point	=	220 F.	104 C.
Thread	=	230 - 234 F.	110 - 112 C.
Soft ball	=	235 - 240 F.	112 - 116 C.
Firm ball	=	244 - 248 F.	118 - 120 C.
Hard ball	=	250 - 266 F.	121 - 130 C.
Soft crack	=	270 - 290 F.	132 - 143 C.
Hard crack	=	300 - 310 F.	149 - 154 C.

SOME AMERICAN-BRITISH TRANSLATIONS

American:	British:
Frosting	Icing
Shortening	Baking lard
Confectioners', powdered sugar	Icing sugar
Graham-cracker, vanilla wafers	Digestive biscuits
Cookie	Biscuit
Molasses	Treacle

All spoonfuls to be considered level unless otherwise specified.

*Grams are rounded
**Centigrade temperatures are rounded

INDEX OF ILLUSTRATIONS